DATE DUE

GAYLORD			PRINTED IN U.S.A.

IN THE
Canon's
MOUTH

LILLIAN S. ROBINSON

IN THE
Canon's
MOUTH

dispatches from the culture wars

INDIANA UNIVERSITY PRESS

bloomington and indianapolis

The paper used in this publication meets the minimum requirements of American National Standard for Information Sciences—Permanence of Paper for
Printed Library Materials, ANSI Z39.48-1984.

Manufactured in the United States of America

Library of Congress Cataloging-in-Publication Data

Robinson, Lillian S.
    In the Canon's mouth : dispatches from the culture wars / Lillian S.
Robinson.
        p.   cm.
    Includes bibliographical references and index.
    ISBN 0-253-33309-1 (alk. paper). — ISBN 0-253-21134-4 (pbk. :
alk. paper)
    1. American literature—History and criticism—Theory, etc.
2. Canon (Literature)   3. Culture conflict—United States.
4. Multiculturalism—United States.   5. Literature and society—
United States—History—20th century.   6. Feminism and literature—
United States—History—20th century.   7. Criticism—United States—
History—20th century.   8. American literature—Study and teaching—
United States.   9. United States—Intellectual life—20th century.
10. English literature—History and criticism—Theory, etc.
I. Title.
PS25.R63   1997
810.9—dc21   97-1670

             1 2 3 4 5   02 01 00 99 98 97

In Loving Memory
of
Constance Coiner
(1948–1996)

"Are you there, girlfriend . . . ?"

CONTENTS

ACKNOWLEDGMENTS

Further bibliographical information is provided in the head-note on each of the previously published articles or reviews in this collection. I am very grateful to the copyright holders for permission to reprint the following pieces:

"The Practice of Theories: An Immodest Proposal"
> Reprinted by permission from *Concerns*/Women's Caucus for the Modern Languages.

"Firing the Literary Canons"
> Reprinted with permission from *Insight on the News*. © 1994 *Insight*. All rights reserved.

"What Culture Should Mean," *The Nation* magazine. © 1989 The Nation Company, LP. Reprinted with permission.

"I, Too, Am America—I," *The Nation* magazine. © 1990 The Nation Company, LP. Reprinted with permission.

"Canon Fathers and Myth Universe"
> Reprinted with permission from *New Literary History*.

"'The Great Unexamined': Silence, Speech, and Class," from *Listening to Silences: New Essays in Feminist Criticism*, edited by Elaine Hedges and Shelley Fisher Fishkin. © 1994 by Oxford University Press, Inc. Reprinted by permission.

"Treason Our Text: Feminist Challenges to the Literary Canon"
"Feminist Criticism: How Do We Know When We've Won?"
"Is There Class in This Text?"
> All reprinted by permission from *Tulsa Studies in Women's Literature*.

Many individuals helped bring these pieces into being, get them ready for publication, or find an audience for them. Special thanks go to Julie Abraham, Margot Backus, James R. Bennett, Shari Benstock, Ryan Bishop, Ellen Cantarow, Rhoda Channing, Ralph Cohen, Mary DeShazer, Elsa Dixler, Moira Ferguson, Shelley Fisher Fishkin, Linda Gardiner, Elaine Hedges, Jeanne Holland,

Natalie Kampen, Holly Laird, Paul Lauter, Peggy McIntosh, Jane Marcus, Elizabeth Meese, Julien Murphy, Alice Parker, Sonia Saldívar-Hull, Ruth Perry, Carol Sternhell, Michelle Tokarczyk, Kazuko Watanabe, Mie Watanabe, Gay Wilentz, and Marilyn Yalom.

The editorial staff at Indiana University Press has made it a pleasure as well as an honor to be on their list. Special thanks to Joan Catapano, the sponsoring editor, Terry L. Cagle, Managing Editor, who oversaw production, and Stephanie G'Schwind, a copy editor who really knows how to read.

For collegial support and encouragement, this project owes much to Marie Farr, Robin Martin, Rick Taylor, Gay Wilentz, and Jeff Williams. For nurturance, both metaphorical and concrete, my loving thanks to Ryan Bishop, the brilliant collaborator on my *next* book; to Shelley Fisher Fishkin, Jane Marcus, and Tillie Olsen, the most inspiring friends any scholar and writer could have; Michael Massing and Dale Williamson, my invaluable assistants; Greg Robinson, my resourceful nephew; and Alex Robinson-Gilden, my matchless son.

DISPATCHES

Introduction

This book is not really finished. The contents are salvos, short bursts of fire from the complex of formative incidents we call the culture wars. And the process, the war, continues. Today's headlines tell me reactionary alumni are organizing nationally to protest the opening of the literary curriculum, one of the projects to which I've devoted my life. *Bring back Shakespeare*, they're apparently chanting out there. *No more postmodern, postcolonial, multicultural, feminist, queer courses that aren't really literature, but psychology, sociology, (gasp) politics.*[1] I sigh and prepare to shoot off another letter, article, lecture in which I poke fun at and holes in this sudden devotion to the Swan of Avon. Whereas I, the "Shakespeare-basher," really like the stuff. I just don't want. . . . Well, it's all over this book, what I think and want and don't want about culture and education, even though—necessarily—it takes the form of brief dispatches from the front.

Instead of after-the-fact memoirs or a single, smooth, integrated argument, *In the Canon's Mouth* brings together articles, reviews, and lectures I wrote between 1982 and 1996 on some of the issues that constitute the battleground of the culture wars: curriculum change, multiculturalism, feminism, political correctness. Given the accelerated pace of intellectual history in the postmodern moment, it's the rare collection that would still seem timely with contents dating back eight, a dozen, fourteen years. If this one does, it's because the issues and the underlying power struggle remain unresolved. In fact, it is the earliest of these pieces that has been reprinted most often and most recently.

Some of the previously published material appeared in academic journals (*New Literary History, Tulsa Studies in Women's Literature*), some in publications that create bridges between feminism and the academy (*Concerns, Women's Review of Books*), and some in magazines of opinion on the left (*The Nation*) and the right (*Insight on the News*). In editing all of them for publication, I have resisted the urge to alter them in the light of subsequent developments and the brilliant hindsight those developments afford. But, whenever possible, I have deleted what were, in their original sites, intentional repetitions and citations of other pieces that are now between the same covers.

Versions of the lectures entitled "In the Canon's Mouth" and "Waving the Flag at Racism and Sexism" have been presented at more than twenty-five colleges and universities in this country, as well as in Japan, Mexico, and Thailand. By contrast, "The Culture, Stupid," the last piece in the collection, was conceived as a lecture, a companion piece for "Waving the Flag at Racism and Sexism," but it has never actually been delivered in its entirety.[2]

Certain other educational experiences simultaneously draw on and contribute to my thinking about the making and teaching of "culture." In June 1992, for instance, I was part of the team that taught a two-week intensive graduate course on North American Identity from a multicultural perspective at the Universidad Nacional Autónoma in Mexico City.[3] Later that summer, I taught a month-long Graduate Institute on The Canon and Popular Genres at the University of Tulsa. Early in 1993, the United States Information Agency sent me to Thailand to keynote a conference for college English teachers on "Changing Directions in the Study of American Literature," asking me to stress the introduction of multicultural and feminist approaches into the curriculum.

What I am trying to say is that I have been living with these issues and discussing them with a variety of audiences for some time now—so long that one of the central concepts with which I work, "the politics of" whatever I'm talking about (the literary curriculum, university speech codes, censorship of the arts, dumbed-down literature anthologies), has completely changed its meaning. In one sense, the limits of political discourse have decidedly narrowed over the past two decades. On the other hand, at least it is no longer necessary to point out that the subject is indeed "the politics of," because the culture wars underscore the connections between the campus and the rest of the world. Pat Buchanan and

Jesse Helms, whose status as political professionals is unquestionable, are fighting the culture wars, chiefly on issues of religion, the arts, mass media, and sexualities, and, when I engage the same issues on my own turf, the politics can no longer be muted on this side, either. Everyone, nowadays, accepts that when we are talking culture, we are talking politics.

When I refer to my turf, I mean the university and the teaching of literature within it. Yet, having resigned from a tenured position, throughout most of the fourteen years in which these articles, reviews, and lectures were produced, I had no permanent academic job. I did go first class when I went at all, setting my *tuchus* on a record number of named Chairs—five of them—as well as holding other visiting positions and fellowships. But the periods between were supported by non-academic jobs, freelance writing and translating, food stamps, and, ironically, campus tours featuring, among others, the lectures reprinted here. I have been at once an exponent, an embodiment, and a victim of the struggle over what we mean (or mean to mean or should mean) when we talk about culture. The experience has given me a unique perspective on educational issues, as someone who both is and is not part of the academic world. I have not had the opportunity to make a continuing impact on the policies and practices of a single institution or to work consistently with the same students. But unemployment freed me to do more writing and lecturing and thereby to be heard on many more campuses. My peripatetic teaching career has brought me to large and small institutions, public and private, denominational and secular, coeducational and single-sex, with highly selective and open admissions standards. So I have seen the curricular and social—in fact, the cultural—forms these issues assume in different environments. And, at least, the populist right can hardly call my experience "elitist" or "ivory tower."

Jane Marcus's wonderful essay "The Proper Upkeep of Names" elaborates on the significance of the "But" with which Virginia Woolf begins *A Room of One's Own*.[4] I would have liked to end this book with that word. In *my* context, it not only represents the challenge to authority that Woolf effected, it also expresses the absence of resolution and closure still inherent in the issues themselves. But . . .

NOTES

1. See Deb Riechmann, "Alumni Stir a Tempest on Literature Classes," *Raleigh News & Observer*, May 2, 1996, 10A.

2. This is no longer true. In October 1996, St. John Fisher College hosted the paper's first full presentation. With less than four days' notice, Margot Backus obtained the generous support of her dean and the English department for a catered luncheon where I could meet with a warm, responsive audience. I made that stop at the Fisher campus en route to a memorial for Constance Coiner, to whom this book is dedicated. The fee for my lunch-time talk is being donated to the lecture series in Coiner's honor that SUNY/Binghamton has established.

3. The others were Gloria Anzaldúa, Shelley Fisher Fishkin, Carla Peterson, Jeffrey Rubin-Dorsky, and Richard Yarborough.

4. Jane Marcus, "Cambridge, Woolf, and *A Room of One's Own*: The Proper Upkeep of Names," Bloomsbury Pamphlets series (London: Cecil Woolf, 1996).

IN THE
Canon's
MOUTH

As a publishing scholar and critic, I've been very lucky in that, over a quarter of a century, I've had only three articles or reviews rejected. "Treason Our Text" is one of them, returned, like the others, by the editor who had originally solicited it. I wrote it in 1982 for the special "Canons" issue of *Critical Inquiry,* for which it was turned down on the grounds that it was too much a survey and was, moreover, inappropriately forceful and ironic in tone! In the meantime, I had presented the piece at the Mellon Seminar at Wellesley's Center for Research on Women, where its reception convinced me that it did have an audience. This experience encouraged me to offer it, the next semester, to Shari Benstock, who, as the new editor of *Tulsa Studies in Women's Literature,* had just invited me to join that journal's editorial board. So, in 1983, it came out almost simultaneously in volume 2 of *Tulsa Studies* and as number 105 in the Wellesley Center's Working Papers series. Thereafter, it was reprinted six times between 1984 and 1994, including a translation into Hungarian, and a Spanish version is now in press, all of this suggesting that not everyone agrees that its force and irony were misplaced. Because it has appeared in three general—that is, non-feminist—collections of contemporary critical theory, it is the piece I am best known for among male readers. Lest this go to my head, I recall a charming postcard I received a few years back from Kathleen Gregory Klein, who told me she'd cited the article at a conference of drama specialists unfamiliar with the title. They all heard it as "Trees in Our Text."

TREASON

Feminist Challenges to the Literary Canon

OUR TEXT

> Successful plots have often had gunpowder
> in them. Feminist critics have gone so far as
> to take treason to the canon as our text.
> —Jane Marcus[1]

The lofty seat of canonized bards (Pollok, 1827).

As with many other restrictive institutions, we are hardly aware
of it until we come into conflict with it; the elements of the literary
canon are simply absorbed by the apprentice scholar and critic in
the normal course of graduate education, without anyone's ever
seeming to inculcate or defend them. Appeal, were any necessary,
would be to the other meaning of "canon," that is, to established
standards of judgment and of taste. Not that either definition is presented as rigid and immutable—far from it, for lectures in literary
history are full of wry references to a benighted though hardly distant past when, say, the metaphysical poets were insufficiently appreciated or Vachel Lindsay was the most modern poet recognized
in American literature. Whence the acknowledgement of a subjective dimension, sometimes generalized as "sensibility," to the category of taste. Sweeping modifications in the canon are said to occur
because of changes in collective sensibility, but individual admis-

sions and elevations from "minor" to "major" status tend to be achieved by successful critical promotion, which is to say, demonstration that a particular author does meet generally accepted criteria of excellence.

The results, moreover, are nowhere codified: they are neither set down in a single place, nor are they absolutely uniform. In the visual arts and in music, the cold realities of patronage, purchase, presentation in private and public collections, or performance on concert programs create the conditions for a work's canonical status or lack of it. No equivalent set of institutional arrangements exists for literature, however. The fact of publication and even the feat of remaining in print for generations, which are at least analogous to the ways in which pictures and music are displayed, are not the same sort of indicators; they represent less of an investment and hence less general acceptance of their canonicity. In the circumstances, it may seem somewhat of an exaggeration to speak of "the" literary canon, almost paranoid to call it an institution, downright hysterical to characterize that institution as restrictive. The whole business is so much more informal, after all, than any of these terms implies, the concomitant processes so much more gentlemanly. Surely, it is more like a gentlemen's agreement than a repressive instrument—isn't it?

But a gentleman is inescapably—that is, by definition—a member of a privileged class and of the male sex. From this perspective, it is probably quite accurate to think of the canon as an entirely gentlemanly artifact, considering how few works by non-members of that class and sex make it into the informal agglomeration of course syllabi, anthologies, and widely-commented upon "standard authors" that constitutes the canon as it is generally understood. For, beyond their availability on bookshelves, it is through the teaching and study—one might even say the habitual teaching and study—of certain works that they become institutionalized as canonical literature. Within that broad canon, moreover, those admitted but read only in advanced courses, commented upon only by more or less narrow specialists, are subjected to the further tyranny of "major" versus "minor."

For more than a decade now, feminist scholars have been protesting the apparently systematic neglect of women's experience in the literary canon, neglect that takes the form of distorting and misreading the few recognized female writers and excluding the others. Moreover, the argument runs, the predominantly male authors in the canon show us the female character and relations between the sexes in a way that both reflects and contributes to sexist ideology—an aspect of these classic works about which the critical tradition remained silent for generations. The feminist challenge, although intrinsically (and, to my mind, refreshingly) polemical, has not been simply a reiterated attack, but a series of suggested alternatives to the male-dominated membership and attitudes of the accepted canon. In this essay, I propose to examine these feminist alternatives, assess their impact on the standard canon, and propose some directions for further work. Although my emphasis in each section is on the substance of the challenge, the underlying polemic is, I believe, abundantly clear.

. . . the presence of canonized forefathers (Burke, 1790).

Start with the Great Books, the traditional desert-island ones, the foundation of courses in the Western humanistic tradition. No women authors, of course, at all, but within the works thus canonized, certain monumental female images: Helen, Penelope, and Clytemnestra, Beatrice and the Dark Lady of the Sonnets, Bérénice, Cunégonde, and Margarete. The list of interesting female characters is enlarged if we shift to the Survey of English Literature and its classic texts; here, moreover, there is the possible inclusion of a female author or even several, at least as the course's implicit "historical background" ticks through and past the Industrial Revolution. It is a possibility that is not always honored in the observance. "*Beowulf* to Virginia Woolf" is a pleasant enough joke, but, though lots of surveys begin with the Anglo Saxon epic, not all that many conclude with *Mrs. Dalloway*. Even in the nineteenth century, the pace and the necessity of mass omissions may mean leaving out

Austen, one of the Brontës, or Eliot. The analogous over-view of American literary masterpieces, despite the relative brevity and modernity of the period considered, is likely to yield a similarly all-male pantheon; Emily Dickinson may be admitted—but not *necessarily*—and no one else even comes close.[2] Here again, the male-authored canon contributes to the body of information, stereotype, inference, and surmise about the female sex that is general in the culture.

Once this state of affairs has been exposed, there are two possible approaches for feminist criticism. It can emphasize alternative readings of the tradition, readings that reinterpret women's character, motivations, and actions and that identify and challenge sexist ideology. Or it can concentrate on gaining admission to the canon for literature by women writers. Both sorts of work are being pursued, although, to the extent that feminist criticism has defined itself as a sub-field of literary studies—as distinguished from an approach or method—it has tended to concentrate on writing by women.

In fact, however, the current wave of feminist theory began as criticism of certain key texts—both literary and para-literary—in the dominant culture. Kate Millett, Eva Figes, Elizabeth Janeway, Germaine Greer, and Carolyn Heilbrun all use the techniques of essentially literary analysis on the social forms and forces surrounding those texts.[3] The texts themselves may be regarded as "canonical" in the sense that all have had significant impact on the culture as a whole, although the target being addressed is not literature or *its* canon.

In criticism that is more strictly literary in its scope, much attention has been concentrated on male writers in the American tradition. Books like Annette Kolodny's *The Lay of the Land* and Judith Fetterley's *The Resisting Reader* have no systematic, comprehensive equivalent in the criticism of British or European literature.[4] Both of these studies identify masculine values and imagery in a wide range of writings, as well as the alienation that is their consequence for women, men, and society as a whole. In a similar vein, Mary Ellmann's *Thinking About Women* examines ramifications of the tradition of "phallic criticism" as applied to writers of both sexes.[5] These books have in common with one another and with over-arching theoretical manifestos like *Sexual Politics* a sense of having been betrayed by a culture that was supposed to be elevating, liberating, *and one's own.*

By contrast, feminist work devoted to that part of the Western tradition which is neither American nor contemporary is likelier to be more even-handed. "Feminist critics," declare Lenz, Greene, and Neely in introducing their collection of essays on Shakespeare, "recognize that the greatest artists do not necessarily duplicate in their art the orthodoxies of their culture; they may exploit them to create character or intensify conflict, they may struggle with, criticize, or transcend them."[6] From this perspective, Milton may come in for some censure, Shakespeare and Chaucer for both praise and blame, but the clear intention of a feminist approach to these classic authors is to enrich our understanding of what is going on in the texts, as well as how—for better, for worse, or for both—they have shaped our own literary and social ideas.[7] At its angriest, none of this reinterpretation offers a fundamental challenge to the canon *as* canon; although it posits new values, it never suggests that, in the light of those values, we ought to reconsider whether the great monuments are really so great, after all.

. . . such is all the worlde hathe confirmed and agreed upon, that it is authentique and canonical (T. Wilson, 1553).

In an evolutionary model of feminist studies in literature, work on male authors is often characterized as "early," implicitly primitive, whereas scholarship on female authors is the later development, enabling us to see women—the writers themselves and the women they write about—as active agents, rather than passive "images" or victims. This implicit characterization of studies addressed to male writers is as inaccurate as the notion of an inexorable evolution. In fact, as the very definition of feminist criticism has come increasingly to mean scholarship and criticism devoted to women writers, work on the male tradition has continued. By this point, there has been a study of the female characters or the views on the woman question of every major—perhaps every *known*—author in Anglo-American, French, Russian, Spanish, Italian, German, and Scandinavian literature.[8]

Nonetheless, it is an undeniable fact that most feminist criticism focuses on women writers, so that the feminist efforts to humanize the canon have usually meant bringing a woman's point of view to bear by incorporating writers one by one. The case, here, consists in showing that an already recognized woman author has been denied her rightful place, presumably because of the general devaluation of female efforts and subjects. More often than not, such work involves showing that a woman already securely established in the canon belongs in the first, rather than the second, rank. The biographical and critical efforts of R. W. B. Lewis and Cynthia Griffin Wolff, for example, have attempted to enhance Edith Wharton's reputation in this way.[9] Obviously, no challenge is presented to the particular notions of literary quality, timelessness, universality, and other qualities that constitute the rationale for canonicity. The underlying argument, rather, is that consistency, fidelity to those values, requires recognition of at least the few best and best known women writers. Equally obviously, this approach does not call the notion of the canon itself into question.

We acknowledge it Canonlike, but not Canonicall (Bishop Barlow, 1601).

Many feminist critics reject the method of case-by-case demonstration. The wholesale consignment of women's concerns and productions to a grim area bounded by triviality and obscurity cannot be compensated for by tokenism. True equity can be attained, they argue, only by opening up the canon to a much larger number of female voices. This is an endeavor that eventually brings basic aesthetic questions to the fore.

Initially, however, the demand for wider representation of female authors is substantiated by an extraordinary effort of intellectual reappropriation. The emergence of feminist literary study has been characterized, at the base, by scholarship devoted to the discovery, republication, and reappraisal of "lost" or undervalued writers and their work. From Rebecca Harding Davis and Kate Chopin through Zora Neale Hurston and Mina Loy to Meridel LeSueur and Rebecca West, reputations have been reborn or remade and a female counter-canon has come into being, out of components that were largely unavailable even a dozen years ago.[10]

In addition to constituting a feminist alternative to the male-dominated tradition, these authors also have a claim to representation in "the" canon. From this perspective, the work of recovery itself makes one sort of *prima facie* case, giving the lie to the assumption, where it has existed, that, aside from a few names that are household words—differentially appreciated, but certainly well-known—there simply has not been much serious literature by women. Before any aesthetic arguments have been advanced either for or against the admission of such works to the general canon, the new literary scholarship on women has demonstrated that the pool of potential applicants is far larger than anyone has hitherto suspected.

Would Augustine, if he held all the books to have an equal right to canonicity . . . have preferred some to others?
(W. Fitzgerald, trans. Whitaker, 1849).

But the aesthetic issues cannot be forestalled for very long. We need to understand whether the claim is being made that many of the newly recovered or validated texts by women meet existing criteria or, on the other hand, that those criteria themselves intrinsically exclude or tend to exclude women and hence should be modified or replaced. If this polarity is not, in fact, applicable to the process, what *are* the grounds for presenting a large number of new female candidates for (as it were) canonization?

The problem is epitomized in Nina Baym's introduction to her study of American women's fiction between 1820 and 1870:

> Reexamination of this fiction may well show it to lack the esthetic, intellectual and moral complexity and artistry that we demand of great literature. I confess frankly that, although I have found much to interest me in these books, I have not unearthed a forgotten Jane Austen or George Eliot or hit upon the one novel that I would propose to set alongside *The Scarlet Letter*. Yet I cannot avoid the belief that "purely" literary criteria, as they have been employed to identify the best American works, have inevitably had a bias in favor of things male—in favor of, say, a whaling ship, rather than a sewing circle as a symbol of the human community . . . While not claiming any literary greatness for any of the novels . . . in this study, I would like at least to begin to correct such a bias by taking their content seriously. And it is time, perhaps—though this task lies outside my scope here—to reexamine the grounds upon which certain hallowed American classics have been called great.[11]

Now, if students of literature may be allowed to confess to one Great Unreadable among the Great Books, my own *bête noire* has always been the white whale; I have always felt I was missing something in *Moby Dick* that is clearly there for many readers and that is "there" for me when I read (say) Aeschylus or Austen. So I find Baym's strictures congenial, at first reading. Yet the contradictory nature of the position is also evident on the face of it. Am I or am I not being invited to construct a (feminist) aesthetic rationale for my impatience with *Moby Dick*? Do Baym and the current of thought she represents accept "esthetic, intellectual and moral complexity and artistry" as the grounds of greatness or are they challenging those values, as well?

As Myra Jehlen points out most lucidly, this attractive position will not bear close analysis: "[Baym] is having it both ways, admitting the artistic limitations of the women's fiction . . . and at the same time denying the validity of the rulers that measure these limitations, disdaining any ambition to reorder the literary canon and, on second thought, challenging the canon after all, or rather challenging not the canon itself but the grounds for its selection."[12] Jehlen understates the case, however, in calling the duality a para-

dox, which is, after all, an intentionally created and essentially rhetorical phenomenon. What is involved here is more like the *agony*
of feminist criticism, for it is the champions of women's literature
who are torn between defending the quality of their discoveries and
radically redefining literary quality itself.

Those who are concerned with the canon as a pragmatic instrument, rather than a powerful abstraction—the compilers of
more equitable anthologies or course syllabi, for example—have
opted for an uneasy compromise. The literature by women that
they seek—as well as that by members of excluded racial and ethnic
groups and by working people in general—conforms as closely as
possible to the traditional canons of taste and judgment. Not that
it reads like such literature, as far as content and viewpoint are concerned, but the same words about artistic intent and achievement
may be applied without absurdity. At the same time, the rationale
for a new syllabus or anthology relies on a very different criterion:
that of truth to the culture being represented, the *whole* culture
and not the creation of an almost entirely male white elite. Again,
no one seems to be proposing—aloud—the elimination of *Moby
Dick* or *The Scarlet Letter*, just squeezing them over somewhat to
make room for another literary reality, which, joined with the existing canon, will come closer to telling the (poetic) truth.

The effect is pluralist, at best, and the epistemological assumptions underlying the search for a more fully representative literature are strictly empiricist: by including the perspective of women
(who are, after all, half-the-population), we will "know more"
about the culture as it actually was. No one suggests that there
might be something in this literature itself that challenges the values and even the validity of the previously all-male tradition. There
is no reason why the canon need speak with one voice or as one
man on the fundamental questions of human experience. Indeed,
even as an elite white male voice, it can hardly be said to do so.
Yet a commentator like Baym has only to say "it is time, perhaps . . .
to reexamine the grounds," *while not proceeding to do so,* for feminists
to be accused of wishing to "throw out" the entire received culture.

The argument could be more usefully joined, perhaps, if there *were* a current within feminist criticism that went beyond insistence on representation to consideration of precisely how inclusion of women's writing alters our view of the tradition. Or even one that suggested some radical surgery on the list of male authors usually represented.

After all, when we turn from the construction of pantheons, which have no *prescribed* number of places, to the construction of course syllabi, then something does have to be eliminated each time something else is added, and here ideologies, aesthetic and extra-aesthetic, do necessarily come into play. Is the canon and hence the syllabus based on it to be regarded as the compendium of excellence or as the record of cultural history? For there comes a point when the proponent of making the canon recognize the achievement of both sexes has to put up or shut up; either a given woman writer is "good" enough to replace some male writer on the prescribed reading list or she is not. If she is not, then either she should replace him anyway, in the name of telling the truth about the culture, or she should not, in the (unexamined) name of excellence. This is the debate that will have to be engaged and that has so far been broached only in the most "inclusionary" of terms. It is ironic that in American literature, where attacks on the male tradition have been most bitter and the reclamation of women writers so spectacular, the appeal has still been only to pluralism, generosity, and guilt. It is populism without the politics of populism.

To canonize your owne writers (Polimanteria, 1595).

Although I referred earlier to a feminist counter-canon, it is only in certain rather restricted contexts that literature by women has in fact been explicitly placed "counter" to the dominant canon. Generally speaking, feminist scholars have been more concerned with establishing the existence, power, and significance of a specifically *female* tradition. Such a possibility is adumbrated in the title of Patricia Meyer Spacks's *The Female Imagination*; however, this book's overview of selected themes and stages in the female life-cycle as treated by some women writers neither broaches nor (obviously) suggests an answer to the question of whether there is "a" female imagination and what characterizes it.[13]

Somewhat earlier, in her anthology of British and American women poets, Louise Bernikow had made a more positive assertion of a continuity and connection subsisting among them.[14] She leaves it to the poems, however, to forge their own links, and, in a collection that boldly and incisively crosses boundaries between published and unpublished writing, literary and anonymous authorship, "high" art, folk art, and music, it is not easy for the reader to identify what the editor believes it is that makes women's poetry specifically "*women's.*"

Ellen Moers centers her argument for a (transhistorical) female tradition upon the concept of "heroinism," a quality shared by women writers over time with the female characters they created.[15] Moers also points out another kind of continuity, documenting the way that women writers have read, commented on, and been influenced by the writings of other women who were their predecessors or contemporaries. There is also an unacknowledged continuity between the writer and her female reader. Elaine Showalter conceives the female tradition, embodied particularly in the domestic and sensational fiction of the nineteenth century, as being carried out through a kind of subversive conspiracy between author and audience.[16] Showalter is at her best in discussing this minor "women's fiction." Indeed, without ever making a case for popular genres as serious literature, she bases her arguments about a tradition more solidly on them than on acknowledged major figures like Virginia Woolf. By contrast, Sandra Gilbert and Susan Gubar focus almost exclusively on key literary figures, bringing women writers and their subjects together through the theme of perceived female aberration—in the act of literary creation itself, as well as in the behaviors of the created persons or personae.[17]

Moers's vision of a continuity based on "heroinism" finds an echo in later feminist criticism that posits a discrete, perhaps even autonomous "women's culture." The idea of such a culture has been developed by social historians studying the "homosocial" world of nineteenth-century women.[18] It is a view that underlies, for example, Nina Auerbach's study of relationships among women in selected novels, where strong, supportive ties among mothers, daughters, sisters, and female friends not only constitute the real history in which certain women are conceived as living, but function as a normative element as well.[19] That is, fiction in which positive relations subsist to nourish the heroine comes off much better, from Auerbach's point of view, than fiction in which such relations do not exist.

In contrast, Judith Lowder Newton sees the heroines of women's fiction as active, rather than passive, precisely because they do live in a man's world, not an autonomous female one.[20] Defining their power as "ability," rather than "control," she perceives "both a preoccupation with power and subtle power strategies" being exercised by the women in novels by Fanny Burney, Jane Austen, Charlotte Brontë, and George Eliot. Understood in this way, the female tradition, whether or not it in fact reflects and fosters a "culture" of its own, provides an alternative complex of possibilities for women, to be set beside the pits and pedestals offered by all too much of the Great Tradition.

Canonize such a multifarious Genealogie of Comments
(Nashe, 1593).

Historians like Smith-Rosenberg and Cott are careful to specify that their generalizations extend only to white middle- and upper-class women of the nineteenth century. Although literary scholars are equally scrupulous about the national and temporal boundaries of their subject, they tend to use the gender term comprehensively. In this way, conclusions about "women's fiction" or "female consciousness" have been drawn or jumped to from considering a body of work whose authors are all white and comparatively privileged. Of the critical studies I have mentioned, only Bernikow's anthology, *The World Split Open*, brings labor songs, black women's blues lyrics, and anonymous ballads into conjunction with poems that were written for publication by professional writers, both black and white. The other books, which build an extensive case for a female tradition that Bernikow only suggests, delineate their subject in such a way as to exclude not only black and working-class authors, but any notion that race and class might be relevant categories in the definition and apprehension of "women's literature." Similarly, even for discussions of writers who were known to be lesbians, this aspect of the female tradition often remains unacknowledged; worse yet, some of the books that develop the idea of a female tradition are openly homophobic, employing the word "lesbian" only pejoratively.[21]

Black and lesbian scholars, however, have directed much less energy to polemics against the feminist "mainstream" than to concrete, positive work on the literature itself. Recovery and reinterpretation of a wealth of unknown or undervalued texts has suggested the existence of both a black women's tradition and a lesbian tradition. In a clear parallel with the relationship between women's literature in general and the male-dominated tradition, both are by definition part of women's literature, but they are also distinct from and independent of it.

There are important differences, however, between these two traditions and the critical effort surrounding them. Black feminist criticism has the task of demonstrating that, in the face of all the obstacles a racist and sexist society has been able to erect, there is a continuity of black women who have written and written well. It is a matter of gaining recognition for the quality of the writing itself and respect for its principal subject, the lives and consciousness of black women. Black women's literature is also an element of black literature as a whole, where the recognized voices have usually been male. A triple imperative is therefore at work: establishing a discrete and significant black female tradition, then situating it within black literature, and (along with the rest of that literature), within the common American literary heritage.[22] So far, unfortunately, each step toward integration has met with continuing exclusion. A black women's tradition has been recovered and reevaluated, chiefly through the efforts of black feminist scholars. Only some of that work has been accepted as part of either a racially mixed women's literature or a two-sex black literature. As for the gatekeepers of American literature "in general," how many of them, in 1983, are willing to swing open the portals even for Zora Neale Hurston or Paule Marshall? How many have heard of them?

The issue of "inclusion," moreover, brings up questions that echo those raised by opening the male-dominated canon to women. How do generalizations about women's literature "as a whole" change when the work of black women is not merely added to but fully incorporated into that tradition? How does our sense of black literary history change? And what implications do these changes have for reconsideration of the American canon?

Whereas many white literary scholars continue to behave as if there were no major black women writers, most are prepared to admit that certain well-known white writers were lesbians for all or part of their lives. The problem is getting beyond a position that says either "so *that's* what was wrong with her!" or, alternatively, "it doesn't matter who she slept with—we're talking about literature." Much lesbian feminist criticism has addressed theoretical questions about *which* literature is actually part of the lesbian tradition, all writing by lesbians, for example, or all writing by women about women's relations with one another. Questions of class and race enter here as well, both in their own guise and in the by-now familiar form of "aesthetic standards." Who speaks for the lesbian community: the highly educated experimentalist with an unearned income or the naturalistic working-class autobiographer? Or are both the *same kind* of foremother, reflecting the community's range of cultural identities and resistance?[23]

. . . a cheaper way of Canon-making in a corner (Baxter, 1659).

It is not only members of excluded social groups, however, who have challenged the fundamentally elite nature of the existing canon. "Elite" is a literary as well as a social category. It is possible to argue for taking all texts seriously as texts without arguments based on social oppression or cultural exclusion, and popular genres have therefore been studied as part of the female literary tradition. Feminists are not in agreement as to whether domestic and sentimental fiction, the female Gothic, the women's sensational novel functioned as instruments of expression, repression, or subversion, but they have successfully revived interest in the question as a legitimate cultural issue.[24] It is no longer automatically assumed that literature addressed to the mass female audience is necessarily bad because it is sentimental or, for that matter, sentimental because it is addressed to that audience. Feminist criticism has examined without embarrassment an entire literature that was previously dismissed solely because it was popular with women and affirmed standards and values associated with femininity. And proponents of the "continuous tradition" and "women's culture" positions have insisted that this material be placed beside women's "high" art as part of the articulated and organic female tradition.

This point of view remains controversial within the orbit of women's studies, but the real problems start when it comes into contact with the universe of canon-formation. Permission may have been given the contemporary critic to approach a wide range of texts, transcending and even ignoring the traditional canon. But in a context where the ground of struggle—highly contested, moreover—concerns Edith Wharton's advancement to somewhat more major status, fundamental assumptions have changed very little. Can Hawthorne's "d—d mob of scribbling women" *really* be invading the realms so long sanctified by Hawthorne himself and his brother-geniuses? Is this what feminist criticism or even feminist cultural history means? Is it—to apply some outmoded and deceptively simple categories—a good development or a bad one?

If these questions have not been raised, it is because women's literature and the female tradition tend to be evoked as an autonomous cultural experience, not impinging on the rest of literary history.

Wisdome vnder a ragged coate is seldome canonicall (Crosse, 1603).

Whether dealing with popular genres or high art, commentary on the female tradition usually has been based on work that was published at some time and was produced by professional writers. But feminist scholarship has also pushed back the boundaries of literature in other directions, considering a wide range of forms and styles in which women's writing—especially that of women who did not perceive themselves as writers—appears. In this way, women's letters, diaries, journals, autobiographies, oral histories, and private poetry have come under critical scrutiny as evidence of women's consciousness *and expression.*

Generally speaking, feminist criticism has been quite open to such material, recognizing that the very conditions that gave many women the impetus to write made it impossible for their culture to define them as writers. This acceptance has expanded our sense of possible forms and voices, but it has not challenged our received sense of appropriate style. What it amounts to is that if a woman writing in isolation and with no public audience in view nonetheless had "good"—that is, canonical—models, we are impressed with the strength of her text when she applies what she has assimilated about writing to her own experiences as a woman. If, however, her literary models were chosen from the same popular literature that some critics are now beginning to recognize as part of the female tradition, then she has not got hold of an expressive instrument that empowers her.

At the Modern Language Association meetings in 1976, I included in my paper the entire two-page autobiography of a participant in the Summer Schools for Women Workers held at Bryn

Mawr in the first decades of the century. It is a circumstantial narrative in which events from the melancholy to the melodramatic are accumulated in a serviceable, somewhat hackneyed style. The anonymous "Seamer on Men's Underwear" had a unique sense of herself both as an individual and as a member of the working class. But was she a writer? Part of the audience was as moved as I was by the narrative, but the majority was outraged at the piece's failure to meet the criteria—particularly, the "complexity criteria"—of good art.

When I developed my remarks for publication, I wrote about the problems of dealing with an author who is trying too hard to write elegantly and I attempted to make the case that "clichés or sentimentality need not be signals of meretricious prose, and that ultimately it is honest writing for which criticism should be looking."[25] Nowadays, I would also address the question of the female tradition, the role of popular fiction within it, and the influence of that fiction on its audience. It seems to me that, if we accept the work of the professional "scribbling woman," we have also to accept its literary consequences, not drawing the line at the place where that literature may have been the force which enabled an otherwise inarticulate segment of the population to grasp a means of expression and communication.

Once again, however, the arena is the female tradition itself. If we are thinking in terms of canon-formation, it is the alternative canon. Until the aesthetic arguments can be fully worked out in the feminist context, it will be impossible to argue, in the general marketplace of literary ideas, that the novels of Henry James ought to give place—a *little* place, even—to the diaries of his sister Alice. At this point, I suspect most of our male colleagues would consider such a request, even in the name of Alice James, much less the Seamer on Men's Underwear, little more than a form of "reverse discrimination"—a concept to which some of them are already overly attached. It is up to feminist scholars, when and as we determine that this is indeed the right course to pursue, to demonstrate that such an inclusion would constitute a genuinely affirmative action for all of us.

The development of feminist literary criticism and scholarship has already proceeded through a number of identifiable stages. Its pace is more reminiscent of the survey course than of the slow processes of canon-formation and revision, and it has been more successful in defining and sticking to its own intellectual turf, the female counter-canon, than in gaining general canonical recognition for Edith Wharton, Fanny Fern, or the female diarists of the Westward Expansion. In one sense, the more coherent our sense of the female tradition is, the stronger our eventual case. Yet, the longer we wait, the more comfortable the women's literature ghetto—separate, apparently autonomous, and far from equal—may begin to feel.

At the same time, I believe the challenge cannot come only by means of the patent value of the work of women. We must pursue the questions certain of us have raised and retreated from as to the eternal verity of the received standards of greatness or even goodness. And, while not abandoning our new-found female tradition, we have to return to confrontation with "the" canon, examining it as a source of ideas, themes, motifs, and myths about the two sexes. The point in so doing is not to label and hence dismiss even the most sexist literary classics, but for all of us to apprehend them, finally, in all their human dimensions.

NOTES

1. Jane Marcus, "Gunpowder, Treason and Plot," talk delivered at the School of Criticism and Theory, Northwestern University, colloquium on "The Challenge of Feminist Criticism," November, 1981. Seeking authority for the sort of creature a literary canon might be, I turned, like many another, to the *Oxford English Dictionary*. The tags that head up the several sections of this essay are a by-product of that effort, rather than of any more exact and laborious scholarship.

2. In a survey of 50 introductory courses in American literature offered at 25 U.S. colleges and universities, Emily Dickinson's name appeared more often than that of any other woman writer: 20 times. This frequency puts her in a fairly respectable twelfth place. Among the 61 most frequently taught authors, only seven others are women; Edith Wharton and Kate Chopin are each mentioned eight times, Sarah Orne Jewett and Anne Bradstreet six each, Flannery O'Connor four times, Willa Cather and Mary Wilkins Freeman each

three times. The same list includes five black authors, all of them male. Responses from other institutions received too late for compilation only confirmed these findings. (See Paul Lauter, "A Small Survey of Introductory Courses in American Literature," *Women's Studies Quarterly*, 9 [Winter 1981]). In another study, 99 professors of English responded to a survey asking which works of American literature published since 1941 they thought should be considered classics and which books should be taught to college students. The work mentioned by the most respondents (59 citations) was Ralph Ellison's *Invisible Man*. No other work by a black appears among the top 20 that constitutes the published list of results. Number 19, *The Complete Stories of Flannery O'Connor*, is the only work on this list by a woman. (*Chronicle of Higher Education*, September 29, 1982.) For British literature, the feminist claim is not that Austen, the Brontës, Eliot, and Woolf are habitually omitted, but rather that they are by no means always included in courses that, like the survey I taught at Columbia some years ago, had room for a single nineteenth-century novel. I know, however, of no systematic study of course offerings in this area more recent than Elaine Showalter's "Women in the Literary Curriculum," *College English*, 32 (1971).

3. Kate Millett, *Sexual Politics* (Garden City, N.Y.: Doubleday, 1970); Eva Figes, *Patriarchal Attitudes* (New York: Stein and Day, 1970); Elizabeth Janeway, *Man's World, Woman's Place: A Study in Social Mythology* (New York: Morrow, 1971); Germaine Greer, *The Female Eunuch* (New York: McGraw-Hill, 1971); Carolyn Heilbrun, *Toward a Recognition of Androgyny* (New York: Harper and Row, 1974). The phenomenon these studies represent is discussed at greater length in a study of which I am a co-author; see Ellen Carol DuBois, Gail Paradise Kelly, Elizabeth Lapovsky Kennedy, Carolyn W. Korsmeyer, and Lillian S. Robinson, *Feminist Scholarship: Kindling in the Groves of Academe* (Urbana and London: University of Illinois Press, 1985).

4. Annette Kolodny, *The Lay of the Land: Metaphor as Experience in American Life and Letters* (Chapel Hill: University of North Carolina Press, 1975); Judith Fetterley, *The Resisting Reader* (Bloomington: Indiana University Press, 1978).

5. Mary Ellmann, *Thinking About Women* (New York: Harcourt, Brace and World, 1968).

6. *The Woman's Part: Feminist Criticism of Shakespeare*, ed. Carolyn Ruth Swift Lenz, Gayle Greene, and Carol Thomas Neely (Urbana: University of Illinois Press, 1980), p. 4. In this vein, see also Juliet Dusinberre, *Shakespeare and the Nature of Woman* (London: Macmillan, 1975); Irene G. Dash, *Wooing, Wedding, and Power: Women in Shakespeare's Plays* (New York: Columbia University Press, 1981).

7. Sandra M. Gilbert, "Patriarchal Poetics and the Woman Reader: Reflections on Milton's Bogey," *PMLA*, 93 (1978), 368–82. The articles on Chaucer and Shakespeare in *The Authority of Experience*, ed. Arlyn Diamond and Lee R. Edwards (Amherst: University of Massachusetts Press, 1977), reflect the complementary tendency.

8. As I learned when surveying fifteen years' worth of *Dissertation Abstracts* and MLA programs, much of this work has taken the form of theses or conference papers, rather than books and journal articles.

9. See R. W. B. Lewis, *Edith Wharton: A Biography* (New York: Harper and Row, 1975); Cynthia Griffin Wolff, *A Feast of Words: The Triumph of Edith Wharton* (New York: Oxford University Press, 1977); see also Marlene Springer, *Edith Wharton and Kate Chopin: A Reference Guide* (Boston: G.K. Hall, 1976).

10. See, for instance, Rebecca Harding Davis, *Life in the Iron Mills* (Old Westbury, N.Y.: The Feminist Press, 1972), with a biographical and critical Afterword by Tillie Olsen; Kate Chopin, *The Complete Works*, ed. Per Seyersted (Baton Rouge: Louisiana State University Press, 1969); Alice Walker, "In Search of Zora Neale Hurston," *Ms.*, 3 (March 1975), 74–75; Robert Hemenway, *Zora Neale Hurston* (Urbana: University of Illinois Press, 1978): Zora Neale Hurston, *I Love Myself When I Am Laughing and Also When I Am Looking Mean and Impressive* (Old Westbury: The Feminist Press, 1979), with introductory material by Alice Walker and Mary Helen Washington; Carolyn Burke, "Becoming Mina Loy," *Women's Studies*, 7 (1979), 136–50; Meridel LeSueur, *Ripening* (Old Westbury: The Feminist Press, 1981); on LeSueur, see also *We Sing Our Struggle: A Tribute to Us All*, ed. Mary McAnally (Tulsa: Cardinal Press, 1982); *The Young Rebecca, Writings of Rebecca West, 1911–1917*, selected and introduced by Jane Marcus (New York: Viking, 1982).

The examples cited are all from the nineteenth and twentieth centuries. Valuable work has also been done on women writers before the Industrial Revolution. See *By a Woman Writt: Literature from Six Centuries by and About Women*, ed. Joan Goulianos (Indianapolis: Bobbs, Merrill, 1973); *The Female Spectator: English Women Writers before 1800*, ed. Mary R. Mahl and Helene Koon (Bloomington: Indiana University Press, 1977).

11. Nina Baym, *Women's Fiction: A Guide to Novels By and About Women in America, 1820–70* (Ithaca: Cornell University Press, 1978), pp. 14–15.

12. Myra Jehlen, "Archimedes and the Paradox of Feminist Criticism," *Signs: Journal of Women in Culture and Society*, 6 (1981), 592.

13. Patricia Meyer Spacks, *The Female Imagination* (New York: Knopf, 1975).

14. *The World Split Open: Four Centuries of Women Poets In England and America, 1552–1950*, ed. and introduced by Louise Bernikow (New York: Vintage-Random House, 1974).

15. Ellen Moers, *Literary Women* (Garden City, N.Y.: Doubleday, 1976).

16. Elaine Showalter, *A Literature of Their Own* (Princeton: Princeton University Press, 1977).

17. Sandra M. Gilbert and Susan Gubar, *The Madwoman in the Attic: The Woman Writer and the Nineteenth-Century Literary Imagination* (New Haven: Yale University Press, 1979).

18. Caroll Smith-Rosenberg, "The Female World of Love and Ritual: Relations between Women in Nineteenth-Century America," *Signs: Journal of Women in Culture and Society*, 1 (1975), 1–30; Nancy F. Cott, *The Bonds of*

Womanhood: "Women's Sphere" in New England, 1780–1830 (New Haven: Yale University Press, 1977).

19. Nina Auerbach, *Communities of Women: An Idea in Fiction* (Cambridge: Harvard University Press, 1979). See also Janet M. Todd, *Women's Friendship in Literature* (New York: Columbia University Press, 1980); Louise Bernikow, *Among Women* (New York: Harmony-Crown, 1980).

20. Judith Lowder Newton, *Women, Power and Subversion: Social Strategies in British Fiction, 1778–1860* (Athens: University of Georgia Press, 1981).

21. On the failings of feminist criticism with respect to black and/or lesbian writers, see Barbara Smith, "Toward a Black Feminist Criticism," *Conditions,* 2 (1977); Mary Helen Washington, "New Lives and New Letters: Black Women Writers at the End of the Seventies," *College English,* 43 (1981); Bonnie Zimmerman, "What Has Never Been: An Overview of Lesbian Feminist Literary Criticism," *Feminist Studies,* 7 (1981).

22. See, for instance, Smith, "Toward a Black Feminist Criticism," Barbara Christian, *Black Women Novelists: The Development of a Tradition, 1892–1976* (Westport, Conn.: Greenwood Press, 1980); *Black Sister,* ed. Erlene Stetson (Bloomington: Indiana University Press, 1981) and its forthcoming sequel; Gloria Hull, "Black Women Poets from Wheatley to Walker," in *Sturdy Black Bridges: Visions of Black Women in Literature,* ed. Roseann P. Bell, Bettye J. Parker and Beverley Guy-Sheftall (New York: Arbor, 1979); Mary Helen Washington, "Introduction: In Pursuit of Our Own History," *Midnight Birds* (Garden City, N.Y.: Anchor-Doubleday, 1980); the essays and bibliographies in *But Some of Us Are Brave,* ed. Gloria Hull, Patricia Bell Scott, and Barbara Smith (Old Westbury: The Feminist Press, 1982).

23. See Zimmerman, "What Has Never Been"; Adrienne Rich, "Jane Eyre: Trials of a Motherless Girl," in *Lies, Secrets, and Silence: Selected Prose, 1966–1978* (New York: Norton, 1979); Lillian Faderman, *Surpassing the Love of Men: Romantic Friendship and Love Between Women from the Renaissance to the Present* (New York: Morrow, 1981); the literary essays in *Lesbian Studies,* ed. Margaret Cruikshank (Old Westbury, N.Y.: The Feminist Press, 1982).

24. Some examples on different sides of the question are: Ann Douglas, *The Feminization of American Culture* (New York: Knopf, 1976); Showalter, *A Literature of Their Own* and her article, "Dinah Mulock Craik and the Tactics of Sentiment: A Case Study in Victorian Female Authorship," *Feminist Studies,* 2 (1975); Katherine Ellis, "Paradise Lost: The Limits of Domesticity in the Nineteenth-Century Novel," *Feminist Studies,* 2 (1975). See also Ellis's "Charlotte Smith's Subversive Gothic," *Feminist Studies,* 3 (1976).

25. "Working/Women/Writing," in Lillian S. Robinson, *Sex, Class, and Culture* (Bloomington: Indiana University Press, 1978; rpt. New York: Methuen, 1986), p. 252.

I sent "Treason Our Text" off on its abortive journey to *Critical Inquiry* at the end of September 1982. By November, when it was time to present it at the Mellon Seminar, I'd been having enough afterthoughts to venture on a kind of pentimento. Since I had done work for a second M.A., in the history of art, between my master's and Ph.D. studies in literature, I had been impressed and delighted with Parker and Pollock's *Old Mistresses*, discussed in some detail here, and wanted to explore the ways that the situation in the visual arts might shed light on the canonical issues in literature. After the Wellesley presentation, I did nothing with the piece until Marilyn Yalom asked my permission to include it in the Working Papers series published by Stanford's Center for Research on Women. It appears as Number 21 in the series. (The Center is now called the Institute for Research on Women and Gender. Apparently, those who were embarrassed by the mildly in-your-face cawing of the acronym CROW have adjusted comfortably to the fact that the acronym for the new name sounds like "earwig.") Since it is without a doubt the least familiar piece in this collection, I was pleased to learn that Indiana University Press's anonymous reader, encountering it for the first time, made a point of listing it as one of her favorites.

THEIR CANON, OUR ARSENAL

Attempts to reform humanities curricula in higher education to reflect the experience of women encounter a number of obstacles. It should come as no surprise—though it is more than a tautology—that one of the chief barriers to change has been the existence and nature of the present curriculum. In those humanistic fields devoted to the study of expressive culture—literature, the visual arts, and music—curriculum tends to be organized around the canon, the set of works that are generally accepted as reflecting the art form at its most excellent. Hence, introductory courses focus on the "Great Books" or on "key monuments" of art and music. In more specialized courses, "greatness" or even "keyness" are somewhat less important. A work may be included because it is representative of a period, trend, or school, even though it is acknowledged as comparatively minor. But minor works are minor only within a recognized canon in which they do have a secure, if limited place. Not only do they share formal characteristics with the major ones, they are also constructed as participating, through the very fact of their endurance and codification, in those qualities of timelessness and universality to which reference is perpetually made as the rationale for canonicity in the arts.

Feminists have tended to approach the canon from one of two directions: they have concentrated on male dominance as evident either in the preponderance of men on the list of those whose productions are considered worthy of serious intellectual attention, or as embodied in the gendered and often gender-biased content of the male works that are so widely studied. In both cases, a set of theoretical questions arises whose answers would serve to inform a consistent and effective feminist strategy in the area of the canon and its relation to curricular reform. These questions have to do with defining whether the feminist challenge to the tradition is meant to challenge canonicity itself and the standards that determine it or simply to demonstrate that the mistreatment and exclusion of women is inconsistent with the values purportedly represented in the humanistic tradition. Are feminists calling the idea of "greatness" itself into question, insisting on radically redefining what comprises it, or just attempting to lend it some internal coherence?

The volume of commentary impinging on this question is much greater in literature than in art or (certainly) in music, in film, or—within the humanities but outside the expressive arts—in philosophy. English and modern languages not only tend to be larger fields but, on the level of curriculum, present a rather more urgent case, because it is far likelier that some course work in these areas will be an undergraduate degree requirement. It may be precisely because there has been so much feminist literary criticism, in fact, that the aesthetic and theoretical problems have been most clearly articulated in literary studies, yet have resisted all attempts at resolution. It seems to me that the work that has been done in art history offers some extremely useful insights into these issues while, at the same time, literary and historical approaches provide a framework within which to understand developments in the visual arts.

Although a great deal of early feminist criticism focused on representations of women in the work of male authors and although, "early," inferentially primitive, as this focus was, it remains fruitful for some critics, feminist textual studies has long been virtually synonymous with the study of women writers. (For reasons I can only speculate about, more of the ongoing feminist work on male authors takes the form of dissertations and conference papers than journal articles and books.) Coming out of such readings, the notions of a female tradition, of "women's culture," of the mass female voice as expressed in private writing are chiefly associated with Anglo-American letters. It is in this framework, moreover, that some feminist scholars have made the case for popular genres from domestic fiction to blues songs as participating in an organic female tradition that also includes work of a more conventionally accepted "literary" cast. Parallel to, but clearly based upon the effort to establish a general female tradition, cases—quite different ones—have also been made for the existence of a black women's tradition and a lesbian tradition.

A number of problems emerge from these three approaches (the male tradition, the female tradition, nontraditional private or popular writing). The increasing tendency to define women's studies in literature as focusing on women writers has left us with an inadequate analysis of the dominant tradition as a vehicle of gender ideology. This is not only a weakness in itself; it weakens a comprehensive feminist critique of the canon and the curriculum based on it. So, as work proceeds on female authors, it is unclear whether, from a feminist point of view, those authors should properly *replace* or *be added to* the male authors who already have canonical status. Is the feminist position that the women's literature being rediscovered is "as good as" the predominantly male work that currently enjoys canonical status or is it, rather, that the entire aesthetic discourse—starting with that word "good," perhaps—is fundamentally challenged by consideration of women's work? Approaching the problem through women characters and the ideology about gender that appears in the male tradition ignores women's own historical agency and consciousness. Yet concentrating on that agency by connecting the woman writer with the women she brings into being on the page or connecting her with the female audience for her writing also prompts a theoretical question that is impossible to answer within the present boundaries of feminist literary study, whether those lines be drawn by an "Anglo-American" or a "French" surveyor. It is here that comparison with the visual arts is most suggestive of fresh directions for thinking about literature.

Although the question of canon formation in literature has recently received a certain amount of theoretical attention, it has chiefly interested those who are pragmatically concerned with curriculum reform. Indeed, the literary canon, which is not, in any case, a formally codified and invariable set of texts, is usually considered to be coextensive with those texts that are included in general or specialized syllabi; to a great extent, "canon" and "curriculum" are synonymous in the field of literature. By contrast, in the visual arts, the nature of the objects in question as well as of the study devoted to them makes the canon a much more definite, almost definitive institution. It is even possible to specify five hundred or a thousand key monuments that all students are expected to be able to identify at sight.[1] The curriculum, even at the graduate level, is thus considerably more rigid than in literature, and is the place where the canon ends up, not where it begins. This is because recognition of canonical status in the visual arts, as, indeed, in music, is not solely or primarily a matter of what is taught in art history or musicology courses. Rather, the conditions under which works in these fields are produced, sold, and assigned material value and prestige forces the feminist commentator away from abstract formal categories and into the comparative sociology of the arts, whence the return to examination of literature and *its* material conditions might be expanded and enriched.

In the visual arts, as in literature, the traditional canon is male dominated. And, as in literature, that domination is not only quantitative, based on the preponderance or exclusivity of male masterpieces, but ideological as well. Western visual art, after all, has had a great deal to "say" about women over the centuries, particularly about the female body and hence about female sexuality. Feminist art historians, like their sister scholars in literature, have devoted most of their energy to the act of intellectual and cultural reappropriation entailed in recovering the works of women artists, asserting their numbers and quality, attempting to define the lost tradition that they may constitute.[2] At least as much as with "women's literature," the history of women artists has remained ghettoized: to precisely the extent that it is recognized as a discrete, autonomous tradition, it continues to be excluded from the canon that supposedly represents our common cultural heritage.

At the same time, a non-elite female tradition has come to be acknowledged and revalued, not only by feminist scholars and writers, but by the women's movement in general and by feminist artists in particular. This continuing vein of women's art comprises the forms that have been classified, often pejoratively, as "crafts." Handicrafts—pottery, embroidery, quilting, weaving, beadwork, and so on—have associations with artisanship and domestic labor; they possess low status in both class and gender terms. It is worth noting, though, that the particular craft forms practiced by women in the West are by no means assigned to women in every culture, nor is the separation itself between crafts and fine art by any means a universal phenomenon. Rather, the hierarchy that subsists in the visual arts is unique to Europe and North America and is inextricably bound up with the cultural and material history of the past four or five centuries.

Natalie Kampen has incisively defined the central conscious and unconscious assumptions of Western art history as a series of hierarchical assertions about what is to be considered better than what:

a) That chronology is essential and that time is fundamentally linear and progressive. b) That competition is part of human nature, as is hierarchic arrangement in the organization of reality. c) [That] Italy is better than Northern Europe, and reality organized in a spatial and geometric way is better than nature unorganized by rational means. c1) [That] Greece is better than Rome, France in the Middle Ages and the 19th century is better than Germany, West is better than East and anything is better than black. c2) [That we are to prefer] big over little, finished over informal, heroic over domestic, aesthetic over political, the individual over the collaborative or cooperative. d) [That] painting is better than sculpture is better than architecture is better than minor arts is better than craft/folk art/utilitarian. Narrative is also better than decorative and tough is better than soft.[3]

Kampen confirms my observation that, in the ordering of art media, those forms designated as "crafts" are at the bottom of the scale. Painting and sculpture jointly occupy the highest level, with painting being the more prestigious and respected of the two. Within painting, there is a further traditional hierarchy of subjects and types, as well as of means. Here, historical and allegorical content rates high, pictures of flowers low; painting in oils on canvas is high, pastels and prints are low. Just as the fine arts, generally, are male territory, while most crafts belong to women, within painting the hierarchy of genre also (unsurprisingly) follows that of gender. Historical subjects and large oils are for men; flower painting, pastels, and prints are for women.

Value is evidently assigned in terms of the spirit's being better than the body, the head better than the hand, the individual act of genius better than the communal effort. Hence, crafts are understood as calling chiefly for manual skill, whereas fine arts demand intellectual endeavor, as well. Moreover, the creator of handicrafts normally remains anonymous, whereas the painting is signed. Generalizing from the relationship of art to crafts in twentieth-century ideology, we may add another hierarchical pair to the list: that which is good for nothing is better than that which is good for something. The beauty of fine arts is held to be sufficient in itself, whereas the beautiful work of the craftsperson normally has a utilitarian function, as well.

My summary of power relations among the art forms themselves is borrowed from *Old Mistresses*, by Rozsika Parker and Griselda Pollock.[4] This exciting study, subtitled *Women, Art and Ideology*, bases its thesis on the relationship between women's status in the critical hierarchy of art forms and genres, on the one hand, and their role in the ideology conveyed by the male-dominated artistic tradition, on the other. In the course of developing their argument, Parker and Pollock demonstrate quite clearly that the problem, despite all the obstacles, is not, in fact, an absence of work by women in the Western artistic heritage. Rather, they maintain, women have produced *and been recognized* in virtually all art forms and media. It is only our contemporary art history that, by fully and uncritically embracing the ideology about women's creative potential implicit in the content of male art, renders women's accomplishments invisible or insignificant. They repeatedly reiterate the point that the passive, objectivized, "naturalized" (which is to say, sexualized) condition of women represented in the male visual tradition is at the root of contemporary devaluation of women's potential as makers of art.[5] A connection should also be drawn between this argument and the devaluing of crafts, including those associated with women, as products and reflections of physical rather than mental or spiritual life.

It seems to me that, despite its brilliant insights, *Old Mistresses* is incomplete. One reason for this is that, while correctly identifying twentieth-century art history as at once a source and a confirmation of social attitudes toward the female as subject and creator of art, the authors do not look beyond the boundaries of the discipline. Art history itself has a history, one with its intellectual roots in German idealist philosophy, and it is worthwhile for anyone involved in criticizing some of its fundamental assumptions and their consequences to explore that relation. Moreover, despite its immaculate philosophical antecedents, art history as a field necessarily maintains close ties to the other institutional forces that influence recognition and judgment in the world of art, forces such as museums, connoisseurship, the marketplace, patronage, and art education. All of these are important factors in the overall situation faced by women on both sides of the canvas, as well as in the parallel universe of feminine "crafts."

A more systematic understanding of both class and historical factors, to which *Old Mistresses* alludes, but which it does not pursue, also serves to illuminate the special situation of women in art as the book elaborates it. Thus, for example, Parker and Pollock assign to the later Middle Ages and early Renaissance a series of far-reaching social transformations in the production and consumption of art: "What changed with the Renaissance was the whole constitution of art practice, with a new identity and social position for the artist, ways of training, functions of art, patrons and decoration."[6] As someone who has done extensive work on the fifteenth and sixteenth centuries, I hope it will not be put down to sectarian pedantry if I insist on referring to the Renaissance *period* and not the Renaissance *tout court*, as if a cultural development could be assigned the same conceptual status as a time period. The Renaissance *as* a cultural development or a cluster of them is itself a result of the principal transformation of the period, the transition from feudalism to capitalism. And it is this transformation that had a profound impact on the history of art and the history of women.

Parker and Pollock emphasize the fact that the radical separation of fine arts from crafts, with its attendant gender division of creative labor, which began in the period of the Renaissance, accompanied the destruction of the medieval artist's workshop. What was henceforth to be recognized as art came to be produced in "studios" by artists, overwhelmingly male, trained in academies of fine arts. At the same time, many of the other items that used to be turned out in the same workshops and by the same hands as pictures and statues came to be either mass-produced in factories, to be made by artisans no longer regarded as artists, or to be the product of women's domestic handicrafts.

The emphasis in *Old Mistresses* is, of course and quite properly, on this last category. It seems to me worthwhile, however, to consider the relationship of feminine crafts to the other forms of production that arose in early modern Europe. Once we recognize the period in which the process began as that of the transition to the capitalist mode of production, we can bring to bear on it everything else we know about the history of women and their work at the time.[7] Basically, as the home-workshop model of production came increasingly to be overshadowed, in Europe, by the factory and the capitalist marketplace, there arose a separation whereby the home became increasingly marginal as an economic site. The separation of home and marketplace not only parallels the separation between art workshop and art studio, but is in great part coextensive with and even identical to it.

Women's domestic labor became less central, as work that was done in the cash marketplace produced exchange-values, while household work retained only a use-value. Moreover and as a direct consequence, in early capitalism, the increasingly hegemonic bourgeoisie placed a value—a psychological and cultural value, of course—on the leisure of women of that class. Purchased at the expense of servants working for wages, this leisure was the sign of bourgeois affluence, the indication that the husband/father in that household could afford to hire domestic labor, which produced no surplus but rather justified itself economically through enacting the fact that *his* wife and daughters did not have to work. It was probably the first example in capitalist culture where the absence of work assumed an intangible but no less real value. And, in the resulting leisure of the privileged classes, a woman's "work" was her handicrafts, fine sewing, or embroidery, which, of course, took place outside of the market economy and cash exchange, though within the loose confines of continued material utility.[8]

This development anticipates by a few centuries the complex of phenomena, tending in a similar direction, that Thorstein Veblen was to link together under the rubric of "conspicuous consumption."[9] In the industrial capitalist America that Veblen observed, an entire ethic of consumption had grown up around demonstrating one's accession to or continued possession of wealth by means of the acquisition of material objects notable for their having exchange-value without use-value, indeed, perhaps taking on their exchange-value through the very fact of being without use-value.

From this perspective, it is noteworthy that it was in the transition to capitalism that painting and sculpture, though especially the former, began increasingly to be practiced in forms that made them available on an open marketplace. A painting on canvas might be produced with no particular purchaser in view and no patron behind it. It could be stocked, sold, and repeatedly transferred—all of it in a way impossible for, say, the frescoed wall of a church or palace. The art buyer could thus be someone who was accustomed to trading on a cash market, for whom the purchase represented precisely an article of conspicuous consumption, something of no immediate utility, but a known and even increasing exchange-value available in the same marketplace as other durable goods.[10]

In today's market, of course, art is often acquired *chiefly* for its exchange-value, as against even its conspicuous-consumption value. That is, it is acquired as an investment that the purchaser hopes will appreciate in value. In a sense, the further the work of art is abstracted from any relation to utility, the greater the role it plays in the marketplace. This means that the greater the investment potential—the higher, in short, the stakes—the higher the barriers against the work of women artists, which, although usually cheaper now, bears the onus of being unlikely to appreciate spectacularly in value. Such work may also be associated with the non-elite world of women's craft objects, which, even when, as in the current market, they may become collector's items, carry price tags that almost never exceed four figures.[11]

I believe that, generally speaking, Parker and Pollock are right to emphasize the influence of art history as a discipline. But their bias in favor of a continuous female tradition that has been ignored only in our time causes them to give insufficient attention to factors that might support other theses, particularly the factors tending to deny women access to becoming artists at all. The first of these is, of course, access to artistic training. Most of the well-known women artists from the immediate post-Renaissance period through the nineteenth century had unusual access to private instruction, often from a male family member who was already a practicing artist. And Linda Nochlin makes much of the fact that, in the last century, even where women were admitted to academies of art, they were not permitted to study life drawing from the human nude.[12]

Parker and Pollock acknowledge this obstacle but dismiss the issue as "just sociology" when, in fact, it is basic to the major issue they themselves stress, the relationship of artistic content to the status of women as artists. For, as Lise Vogel and I pointed out some years ago, the point Nochlin raises should not be reduced to a simple question of the denial of equal educational opportunity in the arts.[13] The problem is that both male and female students were working in an aesthetic system that blandly rejected the notion that the representation of the nude might have any sexual content or implications and that was moving increasingly toward rejecting the idea that *any* content of art has "meaning" behind its formal dimensions. Yet, at the same time, when it came to the training of female students, the nude body was an "improper" source of instruction for them, which must mean that, in this single instance only, the body took on once again all the qualities and associations that it had in society and that the formalist aesthetic was supposed to ignore.

Acknowledging this contradiction actually strengthens one of Parker and Pollock's arguments, for it is they who point out the existence of the generic hierarchy, with allegorical and historical painting at the top. They do recognize that women artists worked— even pioneered—in other subjects and in other media precisely because most lacked the fundamental training to do the nude figure required by the more prestigious forms. But their subsequent discussion of women's achievement in the other subjects and media tends to mask the fact that those areas were not freely chosen from the full range of possibilities.

Fruitful analogies may perhaps be drawn between this situation and the forms and genres traditionally practiced by women writers—the novel and the lyric poem over drama and the epic, for example—particularly if access to patronage is considered as yet another factor in gaining an identity and a career as an artist. Again, Parker and Pollock acknowledge the existence of the issue, stating that it is a complex problem and one that is insufficiently understood with respect to women, but making no effort to investigate it themselves. In fact, the problem of the material support of the artist while work is being produced—whether that work has been in any sense commissioned or is to brave the open market—is a serious one. The question of investing money in the productions of a woman artist reappears here, as do the difficulties, in a sexist culture, of interpersonal relations between women who work at anything, including art, and men of wealth and power.[14] The same issues also arise with respect to that smaller investment needed to enable an artist to work at all. In today's art world, commissions still exist, normally on the public or corporate level, as does individual patronage. But there are also sources of support through private and public foundations. In each of these arenas, women are less favored than men, and a large portion of the blame must rest with the considerably lower eventual price tag attached to women's work. This, in turn, goes back to the ideology about women and hence women artists that the visual arts themselves have been instrumental in fostering.

The marketplace is inescapable in any discussion of the visual arts, for it is relevant to the question of which works have the primary claim on canonicity, that of being acquired for and shown in museums, along with the supporting evidence that accompanies this claim: purchase by private collectors, command of high prices on sale or resale, and so on. Again, it is useful to compare the absolute nature of the market (absolute, that is, at any given moment, although subject to enormous fluctuations over time) with the relative informality of canon formation and maintenance in literature.

I think that the most important application the literary scholar can make of this comparison is to use it to interrogate the literary equivalents of these market forces and, more particularly, the way in which they influence the reputation of women writers. The material nature of the canon in the visual arts also forces the critic to confront the aesthetic questions that remain unresolved with respect to literature. Facing these questions in art history will make it possible to see the issues of feminist literary criticism in a new and more revealing light. If, by analogy with Parker and Pollock's claim about visual art, the women in the literary text can be materially and conceptually connected to the traditional treatment of the woman writer, then the work of literature acquires depth as a social entity and the process is a further step in the elaboration of an aesthetic that does cover male and female, "high" art and "craft," metropolitan and colonial or "primitive," assigning each an honored and honorable place in the history of human creativity and hence in the canon, which serves to recognize and preserve that history.

NOTES

1. When I passed M.A. comprehensives at the NYU Institute of Fine Arts, the first major section of the exam involved precisely such recognition, based on a book called something very like *Key Monuments of Western Art*, which our eye was supposed to have memorized. For the most familiar key monuments, an unexpected detail would be chosen—an extreme close-up of St. Peter's Basilica, say, or a bird's-eye view of the Paris Opéra.

2. See, for instance, Ann Sutherland Harris and Linda Nochlin, *Women Artists, 1500–1900* (Los Angeles: Los Angeles County Museum, 1975) and Germaine Greer, *The Obstacle Race* (New York: McGraw-Hill, 1979).

3. This list was first enunciated in Natalie Kampen's oral presentation to the Mellon Seminar, Wellesley College Center for Research on Women, on November 2, 1982, at the same session where I presented early versions of both "Treason Our Text" and this paper. The published version of Kampen's talk is available, along with Elizabeth Grossman's contribution to that meeting, under the title "Feminism and Methodology: Dynamics of Change in the History of Art and Architecture" as Number 122 (1983) in the Center's Working Papers series.

4. Rozsika Parker and Griselda Pollock, *Old Mistresses: Women, Art and Ideology* (New York: Pantheon-Random House, 1981).

5. More than a decade after Parker and Pollock issued their challenge to traditional art history, their thesis was stunningly illustrated in Eunice Lipton's study of the artist Victorine Meurent, the model for Manet's *Olympia*. See Eunice Lipton, *Alias Olympia* (New York: Scribners-Macmillan, 1992).

6. Parker and Pollock, p. 17.

7. See, for instance, Joan Kelly Gadol, "Did Women Have a Renaissance?" in *Becoming Visible: Women in European History*, ed. Renate Bridenthal and Claudia Koonz (Boston: Houghton Mifflin, 1979); Joan Kelly Gadol, "Social Relations of the Sexes," *Signs: Journal of Women in Culture and Society*, 1 (1976); and Alice Clark, *Working Life of Women in the Seventeenth Century*, 1907 (rpt. ed. London: Routledge and Kegan Paul, 1982).

8. See Parker and Pollock, chapter 2, "Crafty Women and the Hierarchy of the Arts," pp. 50–81; Rozsika Parker, "The Word for Embroidery was WORK," *Spare Rib*, 37 (1975). Pages 171–75 of *Old Mistresses* contain an excellent Select Bibliography, especially with respect to women's crafts.

9. Thorstein Veblen, *The Theory of the Leisure Class*, 1899, widely reprinted.

10. This development is discussed with special reference to seventeenth-century Dutch painting in an article I co-authored: Lillian S. Robinson and Lise Vogel, "Modernism and History," *New Literary History*, 3 (1971), reprinted in my collection *Sex, Class, and Culture* (Bloomington: Indiana University Press,

1978; New York: Methuen, 1986), pp. 22–46; on this issue, see especially pp. 39–41.

11. Alice Walker's short story "Everyday Use" is the best critique I know of the tendency to make the craft-object a collector's item and (hence) the object of investment.

12. Linda Nochlin, "Why Are There NO Great Women Artists?" *Art News*, 69 (1971), 32–36.

13. Robinson and Vogel, p. 32.

14. See Lucy Lippard, "Women Artists Versus Rich Dead Men," *Village Voice*, December 9, 1982. The title alone is most suggestive—not to say provocative.

At the 1983 MLA meeting in New York, *Tulsa Studies* ran a session on Feminist Issues in Literary Scholarship. The event was meant to mark the journal's transition from its early focus on archival scholarship about women writers to a wider range of critical and theoretical issues. That's why I begin "How Do We Know When We've Won?" with a question about the relation of scholarly research to feminism. Papers by the original panelists—Nina Auerbach, Jane Marcus, Judith Lowder Newton, and me—were supplemented by others to constitute a prize-winning special issue of the journal (Volume 3 [1984]). Further expanded and revised, that group of essays became *Feminist Issues in Literary Scholarship*, edited by Shari Benstock and brought out by Indiana University Press in 1987. My contribution has also been published in a Japanese translation.

How Do We Know When We've Won?

The specific question we have been invited to address here appears, as initially stated, to be either ingenuous to a fault or impossible to answer. This is not a comfortable dilemma to sit on the horns of. Yet, when asked whether it is essential that scholarship on women writers operate within feminist assumptions and with a feminist orientation, one hesitates over the appropriate response. On the one hand, I am committed to an almost reflexive "Yes, of course," that seeks to place the issue beyond discussion. On the other hand, I catch myself saying things like "on the other hand," attempting to redefine the terms of the question and its possible applications for both feminist and literary theory.

Is there a place for research—criticism and scholarship—on women's literature that, while not being explicitly anti-feminist, nonetheless is not explicitly feminist either? What sort of place? And what work (or whose, as we might more candidly express our uneasiness) may properly be characterized as "merely work on women" but not feminist work? Once these matters have been responsibly dealt with, I am afraid my own answer to the original question comes out a far from resounding "Yes, but. . . . " Rather than being as absolute as one—as I—might wish it to be, that answer starts with a limiting case and approaches what I believe to be most necessary in feminist literary scholarship only by a succession of increasingly closer approximations.

We are still at a stage in the institutional politics of these issues where most of us find ourselves having to shout at administrators and colleagues that of *course* there have been enough important women writers—or enough before 1800 or in this national tradition or that, enough black or Chicana writers, enough dramatists or poets—to justify the study and teaching of this material. But if feminist literary scholarship has not yet eliminated all declarations that (aside from the names that are household words) there really are no women writers to speak of, it has made serious inroads into the complacency with which that absence is asserted.

And that is one of the primary and legitimate tasks of such scholarship: simply to make it impossible to ignore women's contribution to both our common and our distinct literary heritages. The principal locus for the debate, of course, is not the face-to-face polemic, however frustrating, enervating, and necessary it may be, but the larger processes of canon formation, critical attention, and curricular reform. The significance of the limiting case, it seems to me, lies in the conclusions that are automatically drawn from the absence of women in the canon or the syllabus typically based on it. If an undergraduate is required to take one course on the Great Books and they all turn out to have been produced by Great Men, that student will very likely also take it as a given that no woman writer is considered to be suitably Great. Worse, the student will probably not give any thought to the matter. If the American literature survey these days includes a few white women, it is not surprising for the student to conclude that black women have failed to wield the pen to any good literary purpose. (The same conclusion is likely to be reached, of course, about a lily-white syllabus purporting to explore *"women's* literature.")

Considering the negative consequences of the absence of women—negative both intellectually and politically—I would conclude from my limiting case that, by contrast, any work that places the study of women writers at the center has an objectively feminist effect. Extending the female canon lengthwise, back into the centuries before the Industrial Revolution, or laterally, to include writers of color, working-class writers, writers of popular "women's fiction," has a feminist effect almost regardless of the nature of the arguments and connections that are made or ignored about the work itself.

Now, there is a name for the theoretical stance that informs the position I am taking here, and it is a pejorative one. Welcoming all such studies, however limited their contribution to an overall feminist analysis or interpretation, on the grounds that they do add something to What We Know, to the (quantitative or factual) truth, is called empiricism. As one is permitted to do in traffic court, I plead "guilty with an explanation." For the empiricism I am espousing is not vulgar empiricism, increasing the Body-of-Knowledge stuff, but, if you will, an enlightened empiricism, originating in and sustained by the conviction that every piece of something that is provided is better than nothing.

But "Better than Nothing" is a most depressing banner to be carrying through the streets in a feminist demonstration. (The only worse one I can think of, in fact, would read "Lesser of Two Evils.") Moreover, it is a particularly incongruous one for me to seem to be lugging since, from my earliest published work, I have been vocal in challenging feminists to create a criticism qualitatively different from the received tradition. Thirteen years ago, I was saying that feminist critics must not remain "bourgeois critics in drag."

Seven years ago, I was saying that working-class women needed no outside apologists to make and justify their literature for them. Four years ago, I was applauding Jane Marcus's trenchant aphorism (wishing I had said it first) about how it is far more important to be Shakespeare's sisters than Bloom's daughters.[1] So am I not contradicting my own most cherished principles in admitting the Better than Nothing position? I hope not, for while including as much work as possible under the potentially feminist rubric, I nonetheless believe that, once the outer limits are defined, there are those successively closer approximations to the *best* work feminists need to do.

On the one hand, as you will not fail to observe, I am still convinced that I know what "the best" feminist work would be. On the other, I am by no means prepared to dismiss all the other work as not feminist. This inclusive imperative derives from my experience as one of five collaborators on a forthcoming study of feminist scholarship in its first decade.[2] My co-authors are an anthropologist, a historian, a philosopher, and a specialist in comparative education. One of the issues we originally planned to address in our book was the distinction between feminist scholarship in our respective disciplines (*our* side) and research in those fields that was "merely" work on women (the opposition, obviously).

In literary studies, such a distinction lies ready to hand and distinctly prior to any invidious discriminations among poststructuralist, Lacanian, Derridean, Marxist, reader-responding, or eclectic approaches to the issues raised by women's writing. There are women authors, and much of the scholarship and criticism devoted to them—and to the best known of them in particular—concentrates on aspects of their work unrelated to their own gender or to questions of gender in their writing. There is certainly a feminist way— or rather several—of understanding Jane Austen's irony or George Eliot's religion or Virginia Woolf's metaphors. But the vast bulk of critical prose annually devoted to such topics tends, more often than not, to do the thing "straight," that is, gender-blind. There might not even be anything necessarily wrong with that. This vast bulk constitutes the literary equivalent of social science work that

makes women the object rather than the subject of, say, some series of statistical observations. Discussing it would, I thought, be my
contribution to our collective analysis of feminist scholarship versus
work on women. From there it could be readily determined which
of these categories was appropriate for the scholarship chiefly devoted to recovering the work of lost women writers of the past.

But as this section of our book progressed, we discovered, painfully and at length, that although we all still had firm ideas about
what was and was not a genuinely feminist endeavor in the areas
we knew best, we could articulate no standards that really worked,
particularly across disciplinary lines. The criteria we established
were either so narrow as to exclude work we otherwise accepted
as feminist or so broad as to include precisely that which we had
considered most questionably so. We were forced to the conclusion
that the intellectual challenge posed by the women's movement in
general and by women's studies in particular is so potent, even
where unacknowledged, that at the present time it creates the historical context within which all discourse on women occurs.

For instance, each of us had also done a statistical analysis of
journal articles, dissertation abstracts, and presentations at scholarly conventions. In literary studies, I had unsurprisingly concluded that far more of these various types of scholarly contributions were devoted to women writers in 1980, the last year in the
survey, than in 1965. Much of this material was in the "merely on
women" category. But the sheer increase in volume is a by-product
of the existence of feminist criticism, both in general and as addressed to these particular writers. Women writers are now more
acceptable as thesis subjects, in a situation where a graduate student
must seek and obtain approval of the topic. It is likelier nowadays
that the centennial or other anniversary of the birth or death of
a major woman writer will be marked by a special journal issue
or a conference. And even when we are properly infuriated that
such a special issue or confabulation has not even solicited a feminist contribution, we can take a certain amount of credit, cold com-
fort though it may be, from the realization that our work in the
aggregate made it happen. Experiences like this, as well as those

trickier cases where commentators who remain well outside the feminist frame of reference or discourse nonetheless reflect some small gleaning from our bountiful harvest, giving some indication that we are not speaking always and only to ourselves, were common to all five of us. Hence, as I say, we were forced to the conclusion that, at the present moment, feminism provides the locus and the context even for work on women that does not bear a directly feminist stamp. I say "forced" advisedly, yet it may not really be such a bad place to find ourselves. For the time being.

Still, still I do worry. Although I am prepared to define the limits so inclusively, I also have a sense of priorities that speaks to me—and, I believe, to us—in the imperative mood. There is an insistence, even an urgency, underlying my sense of what is to be done—along with a terrible fear that that is increasingly what is not being done. I start from the premise that "woman" as a category defined by gender alone and, hence, in contradistinction to the other category so defined, that is, to "man," does have a historical specificity, a different experience or set of experiences, as well as a different consciousness and a different perspective on those experiences that the two sexes share. Empiricism, the inclusion of women in hypothetical canon or pragmatic curriculum, is not enough. A populist insistence on representing all aspects of our culture in canon and curriculum, without admitting the controversies and contradictions aroused by such representation, is not enough. Inclusion of women should radically and fundamentally alter our sense—everyone's sense—of what the overall canon or curriculum is and what it says. All our generalizations about, say, "the" seventeenth century or "the" American national character have to be reexamined in the light of what women's contributions to making up the literature of the various centuries and nations tells us.

The nature and direction of these changes depend on a prior issue, however: the extent to which challenges to the male-dominated canon also entail challenges to the dominant stylistic, thematic, and aesthetic norms. As the archaeological aspect of feminist scholarship is pursued to good purpose, the academic world in general is increasingly likely to admit to us that, yes, after all, there were some women writing in the seventeenth century. But how many of them, we will be asked, we will ask ourselves, were any good? How many of them are good enough to deserve a place in an honest "coed" canon? How many are good enough to deserve to (deep breath) displace some gentleman on "the" syllabus for seventeenth-century literature? These are by no means rhetorical questions; their answers are not obvious. It all depends on what we mean by "good," on how far scholarship alone, simply uncovering the lost or never-heard voices of women of past centuries, suggests or even dictates a new set of aesthetic principles. How do we know that it is as good? Do we leave the definitions untouched and demonstrate—as is clearly possible in certain cases—that a given woman meets all the existing criteria for goodness? Or do we explicitly or implicitly modify the aesthetic compact? Which: explicitly or implicitly? And according to what criteria?[3]

To undertake investigation of the earlier history of women writers without considering the criteria *other than gender* for inclusion in the canon (and hence for these writers' exclusion) is to walk headlong into an elitist quagmire. It may also mean ignoring some of the richest sources of female expressive tradition, as well as all the further implications of that or any tradition. What, for instance, if it turned out that the Countess of Pembroke really wrote *The Countess of Pembroke's Arcadia*? After all, if Shakespeare's sister was an exemplary myth, Sidney's sister was a living reality, a highly cultivated woman, a patroness, and a writer. There is, as far as I know, not a shred of evidence that she wrote the *Arcadia*—at least not single-handed. But what if . . . ? One for our side and a terrific one—but so what? What would it tell us about women or even about women writing? No special case would have to be made to include Mary Sidney's *Arcadia* in the canon—not now. And the gentlemanly study of gentlemanly texts would recover from the shock absolutely unscathed, particularly if Mary Sidney's *Arcadia* were to be subjected, even by feminists, to the currently fashionable approaches of the responding—or anguished or deconstructing— reader; but not if it were to be subjected to an approach that notices phenomena of class and race, as well as gender.

When it is a question of broadening the canon to include popular literature written by and about women for an overwhelmingly female audience, it is well, once again, to be clear about the reasons for proposing *this* material as literature and for placing it beside the traditional (and traditionally male-authored) monuments hallowed by literary history. Is the argument here to be based on representativeness? Or is our common definition of literary excellence due for an overhaul?

Although I spoke earlier and provisionally of woman as a category defined by gender alone, such a definition is a sort of mathematical abstraction; the problem is further compounded when we recognize that the difference of gender is not the only one that subsists among writers or the people they write about. It may not always be the major one. Women differ from one another by race, by ethnicity, by sexual orientation, and by class. Each of these contributes its historic specificity to social conditions and to the destiny and consciousness of individual women. Moreover, these differences are not simply or even primarily individual attributes. They are *social* definitions, based on the existence and the interaction of groups of people and of historical forces. As scholarship—itself primarily or secondarily feminist—reveals the existence of a black female tradition or a working-class women's literature, it is insufficient simply to tack these works onto the existing canon, even the emerging women's canon. Once again, every generalization about women's writing that was derived from surveying only relatively privileged white writers is called into question by looking at writers who are not middle class and white. It may be that some of these generalizations still hold. My suspicion is, however, that most do not. This is even more likely when, say, black women's literature is assimilated into a *general* American canon that was hitherto predominantly white and male. The addition not only enriches the canon, it changes our sense of what the canon is and what it is about.

Here again, the aesthetic issues are at the forefront. In order to add black women's literature to an all white—much less an all white and all male—canon, certain judgments will have had to be made. On what basis are they to be made? Does the received idea of what is "good" literature have to change and how do we get it to do so? Or is "representativeness" of all available voices in the culture to become the only aesthetic?

At present, it seems to me that a curious double standard is in effect whereby only the women's literature produced by middle-class white women is subjected to the full range of critical and analytic apparatus, including all the currently fashionable linguistic and psychological modalities. Literature by women of color and, perhaps, even by working-class white women may be granted some modicum of critical and (even likelier) pedagogical attention, but it is rarely, if ever, included in general discussions of the female tradition, and it is almost never read according to the modish new ways of reading. Instead it is read as social document. As you can imagine, I have no objection to this unless it ignores the fact and the consequences of the fact that non-elite women's writing is nonetheless fiction or poetry or drama or narrative—that it is, in fact, *literature*. And I have no objection to this unless it gives such unexamined primacy to the author's race or class that it fails to observe any other aspect of her experience or her expression.[4]

But what bothers me even more is the implication that only women of color possess a racial identity that has to be understood by the critic, that only working-class women possess a class identity whose consequences need to be studied. In fact, in a society divided not only by racial differences but by racism, all writers have a significant racial identity. In a society wracked by class tensions—acknowledged or not—all have a class identity. Hence it is my contention that all women's literature deserves to be considered in the light of its full range of social, as well as individual, connotations.

Take, for example, the Countess of Pembroke, to whose career I gave a hearty, if fanciful, boost a few paragraphs back. If it were established that the *Arcadia* was not written by her brother to amuse her but by the Countess to amuse *herself*, then how do we read the book? If the many emendations she made from his notes and known intentions were as much her own invention as the older, simpler text onto which they were grafted; if, in short, it had always been her book, in fact as in name, how do we read it? It seems to me obviously absurd to maintain that interpretation of this text could be altered only by the fact of gender rather than by the interlocking facts of *class* and gender.

That Mary Sidney was a woman of wealth, standing, and some political influence, that she was a patroness of (male) writers, as well as the wife and the mother of great patrons, has to be taken into consideration in apprehending the works she did leave us. All this becomes even more significant if that slender *oeuvre* were to be enriched by the addition of a long prose romance. The *Arcadia* embodies the ideology of a powerful class striving for further self-definition and social domination, ideology that involves ethical and political constructs, as well as those specifically regulating the character and relations of the two sexes. In this way, text and author participate in history, and one function of criticism is to situate and understand them there.

It is true that the archaeological work on the female canon excites me rather less than it might because so much of it—necessarily, inevitably—involves digging up the literary remains of the Honourable Miss This and the Countess of That and the (recusant, secretly Jacobite) Lady The-Other. I confess a general preference for Jacobins over Jacobites, whatever their gender. But when it comes to the newly uncovered literature, a large part of my impatience is owing to the bland assumption on the part of scholars that the combined operations of class and gender have no literary consequences worth bothering about. Now, if Lady Pembroke's *maid* had written the *Arcadia* . . . or something.[5] Well, what? Yes, frankly, it would interest me as an expression of the mass female voice, of someone living through class as well as sex oppression, but chiefly because everyone *else* would also be forced to look at its class dimensions. The maid, you see, has a class identity. The Countess and her knightly brother are treated as belonging to the world of literature and hence, in the peculiar late twentieth-century perception, do not. They are "normal"—that is, they possess a brain and a pen and no history. Indeed, the social exception, the individual of leisure and privilege, *becomes* the literary norm. Surely such madness is only enhanced as we accord to women writers, as well as their brothers, a reading that ignores the material and ideological meaning of class.

I am very much disheartened by increasingly hegemonic, essentialist tendencies in feminist scholarship and criticism. Day by day, even that scholarship that is "merely about women" is providing fundamental links in the chain of knowledge, revealing the existence of a wealth of hitherto unknown, unrecognized, or unremembered literature. Our task, the *feminist* task, is to know what to do with that treasure now that, increasingly, it is in our hands.

NOTES

1. The two pieces of my own referred to here are "Dwelling in Decencies: Radical Criticism and the Feminist Perspective," *College English*, 32 (1971), 879–89, based on a paper delivered at the December 1970 Annual Meeting of MLA, and "Working/Women/Writing," in my *Sex, Class, and Culture* (Bloomington: Indiana University Press, 1978; rpt. New York: Methuen, 1986), pp. 223–53, based on a paper delivered at the Annual Meeting of MLA in December 1976; Jane Marcus's remarks were part of a personal communication in the Fall of 1979.

2. Ellen Carol DuBois, Gail Paradise Kelly, Elizabeth Lapovsky Kennedy, Carolyn W. Korsmeyer, and Lillian S. Robinson, *Feminist Scholarship: Kindling in the Groves of Academe* (Urbana: University of Illinois Press, 1985).

3. On this point, see Myra Jehlen, "Archimedes and the Paradox of Feminist Criticism," *Signs, Journal of Women in Culture and Society* 6 (1981), 575–601.

4. Mary Helen Washington discusses the disastrous effects of mechanically dividing a syllabus into white and black women authors, turning each one into an implicit representative or spokeswoman for her race alone, in her article, "How Racial Differences Helped Us Discover Our Sameness," *Ms.*, 10 (September 1981), 60–62, 76.

5. If my fantasy about Sidney's sister owes its existence and shape to Virginia Woolf's creation of Shakespeare's sister, my thinking about Sidney's sister's *maid* is informed by Woolf's discussion of Mercy Harvey in *The Common Reader: Second Series* (1932; rpt. London: Hogarth Press, 1959).

I wrote this review under the impression that it was to appear in a special section of *Tulsa Studies* devoted to *The Norton Anthology of Literature by Women*. Although, once I saw the book itself, my emphasis shifted from its inclusions and exclusions to the larger social function of a book with so many and such glaring mistakes, I still envisaged my review essay as one among several. In the event, Volume 5, Number 2 of *Tulsa Studies* (1986) published only Sandra Zagarell's favorable assessment of the anthology and this one of mine. "The Queens' Necklace" (pp. 67–76) chronicles some of the responses this piece received.

IS THERE CLASS

On The Norton Anthology of Literature by Women

IN THIS TEXT?

I don't know about desert islands, but I am here to tell you that Gilbert and Gubar's *Norton Anthology of Literature by Women* is a wonderful book to be sick in bed with. The providential arrival of my review copy on the very day, last winter, that I came down with the flu informs my enthusiasm for the general project, as well as my harsher attitude toward the way the editors have implemented it. In fact, the particular sense in which this review focuses on class is a result of that initial, literally feverish reading. A bit of contextual—or, more properly, phenomenological—criticism may therefore be in order, by way of introduction.

When I agreed to contribute to this special issue devoted to

NALW, I made the mild academic joke that is now embodied in my title. From a by-no-means comprehensive perusal of other people's copies of the anthology, I assumed I would be concentrating my remarks on the under-representation of working-class perspectives in the selections included, as well as on the editors' even graver *mis*-representation of the ways that class and race intersect with gender in shaping women's lives and work. Then *Tulsa Studies* sent me its last review copy of *NALW*, the fates sent me a temperature too high to ignore, and I got to spend the long Presidents' Day weekend tucked up with nearly 150 women writers. It made me appreciate the editors' accomplishment as no other reading—at least, no other reading I was likely to give the collection—could do. At the same time, it introduced me to an editorial problem that a less intense reading might just possibly have overlooked.

For a day and a half, between actual bouts of sleep and periods of somnolence where old words like "ague" and "tertian fever" chased each other around in my brain, my appreciation was unalloyed. So I still ask myself what *other* collection could have afforded me forty-seven Emily Dickinson poems between the same covers as all of *Jane Eyre* (ideal flu reading, needless to say), all of *The Bluest Eye*, and good long draughts of writers as various as Tillie Olsen, Amelia Lanier, Rebecca Cox Jackson, Virginia Woolf, Stevie Smith, Margaret Atwood, and Lucille Clifton! So what if the selections—of both authors and specific texts—were not always the ones I would have made, if the book was too heavy yet the pages too thin, the type a challenge to an invalid's eyes, the notes intrusive, tendentious, and so frequently off the mark, if not the wall? But, in the end, it was a footnote that brought an end to this idyll.

By late afternoon of the second day, I was able to sit up for longer periods. Leafing idly through *NALW*, I came upon Anne Stevenson's fine poem, "Re-reading Jane," with which I was not familiar. My eye had been caught by the italicized lines from Jane Austen's novels, which Stevenson ("needlework of those needle eyes," indeed!) neatly stitches into her own poem. So the footnotes explaining sources, references, and characters in Austen's work were particularly noticeable and irritating. They were, nonetheless, part of the (perhaps Faustian) compact we enter into when we read a Norton anthology. In the middle of her poem, however, Stevenson has the lines:

> Novels of manners? Hymenal theology!
> Six little circles of hell with attendant humours. (2244)

Footnote four (for which there is, blessedly, if erroneously, no superscript to interrupt the eye) tells us that Hymen was the Greek god of marriage, as if that would help students understand the exquisite parsimony of that "hymenal theology." Note number five, at the end of the following line, tells us that Austen wrote six novels (well, she *completed* six), that the humours "were thought" (by whom? when?) to control a person's psychological makeup, and that there are seven circles of hell in Dante's *Inferno*. So there are, so there are, but then Dante, Virgil, and the reader proceed together to an eighth and a ninth! These deepest circles, harboring false counselors, cheats, and traitors, are an integral part of Dante's scheme (not subject, that is, to Nortonian abridgement or relegation to the limbo of unfinished works, alongside *Sanditon* and *The Watsons*).

Okay, it's an honest mistake and two editors putting together an anthology of this length are entitled to a few. Let Dante, wrapped up as he was in multiples of three and ten and making it all fit together without wrenching the divine sense, spin in his grave— adding a whole new light show to Paradise, perhaps. Anyway, maybe he brought it on himself by structuring the *Purgatorio* around the Seven Deadly Sins. Yes, surely Gilbert and Gubar are entitled, amid all the notes that are pedantic, silly, vague, or misplaced, to a few outright errors. But, asked the convalescent newly awakening within the still-flushed patient, *how many* errors are they allowed? And what do they mean? I started leafing again and found three more mistakes in the space of five minutes. So my second question assumed greater prominence. What *do* all these errors mean?

The ones I randomly found in those first minutes turned out to be an instructive place to begin. In Muriel Spark's 1961 story, "The Fathers' Daughters," the heroine, visiting the Côte d'Azur with her novelist father, worries about money:

> Since the introduction of the new franc it was impossible to tip less than a franc. There seemed to be a conspiracy all along the coast to hide the lesser coins from the visitors, and one could only find franc pieces in one's purse, and one had to be careful not to embarrass Father, and one.... (1862)

The footnote to the words "new franc" defines it as "a new unit of French currency somewhat smaller than the old franc; worth about twenty cents." That was roughly the exchange rate at the time of the revaluation, shortly before the story was published. But, if Gilbert and Gubar's "somewhat smaller" means *worth* somewhat less—and what else could it mean, since noting the fact that the coin is smaller in size, though accurate, would make nonsense of the passage—it is just plain wrong. The new franc, although its value relative to the dollar may fluctuate, is always worth precisely one hundred times *more* than the old, now called the centime. In the last sentence of the headnote on Spark, we are told that this story "slyly satirizes the way in which patriarchal structures dominate both life and letters." It would be nice (I say no more) if the editors had added something about the way Spark interweaves material and moral economies in this story. Students might notice it for themselves, and, if not, their teacher might point out how class serves Spark as both a metaphor and a functional fact. But, however the editors' interpretive role is limited, it does no good to tell us about the new French coinage only to get it backwards!

Then there is Grace Paley's "Enormous Changes at the Last Minute." The young cabdriver-musician who is about to spend his first night with the heroine rummages through her freezer:

> Apple turnovers! You know I have to admit it, our commune isn't working too well. Probably because it's in Brooklyn and the food coop isn't together. But it's cool, they've accepted the criticism. (1922)

Now, what in that delightful paragraph would *you* think required a gloss? Putting tongue firmly in cheek at the pedantry involved, one *might* decide to explain "food coop" for provincial contemporary or supermarket-bound posterity. In that case, one ought not to define it as "cooperative purchase and preparation of food for the commune." A food coop, my colleagues, is an organization—whether store-front, full-service market, or buying club without permanent headquarters—for the cooperative purchase of food. The food so purchased is prepared at home. If "home" is a commune, the food bought at the coop may turn out to be prepared cooperatively, which, however, does not make the house a food coop. In practice, all this works more or less well, as Paley has Dennis suggest, depending on circumstances. Two weeks after my flu weekend, I had the privilege of hearing Paley read this story to an overflow crowd of students at George Mason University in Fairfax, Virginia. That audience got the joke just fine.

Flipping her thumb once more through the fragile pages, this loyal member of the Kutztown, PA, Food Coop stopped at the selection from Lillian Hellman's *Pentimento*. Hellman describes the developing relationship between Helen, her black housekeeper, and Jimsie, a white Harvard student the two have met:

> It was the period of the early student movement and there was a time when he disappeared into Mississippi and came back beaten up around the kidneys, a favorite place, then and now, for a police beating since it doesn't show. Helen moved him in with us for a week. . . . Jimsie was puzzled, uneasy about the fuss she made over him. And her lack of response to the state of the Negro in the South made him stubborn and nagging. It took years for him to know that it had to do with her age and time: her anger was so great, hidden so deep for so long, that it frightened her and she couldn't face it. He didn't understand her at all, in fact, and there was a funny, nice night in which his attempt to explain to her the reasons for the insanity of the Bay of Pigs was hilarious to hear. (1707–08)

An editor of a truly explanatory temperament might have footnoted "early student movement" or made it clear that in 1961 what people disappeared into Mississippi *on* were called Freedom Rides. Gilbert and Gubar apparently consider the Civil Rights references either self-explanatory or trivial, but "Bay of Pigs" comes in for a note. To wit: "A futile and abortive invasion of Castro's Cuba by the U.S. (1961)." It is hard to imagine anyone, pro or con, who would find that an accurate summary of the event. What is worse, although pausing to provide us with these misleading words, the editors fail to unscramble Hellman's syntax so that today's students, most of them unborn in April 1961, might grasp that it is Jimsie who considers the invasion insane, while Helen "didn't like talk like that."

Five minutes, four errors, concerning (respectively) a work of religious poetry, a foreign society, an alternative lifestyle, and the political views of a young sixties' radical. Am I paranoid—or is there a pattern here? There certainly seems, first of all, to be an area of gross insensitivity when it comes to the Judeo-Christian tradition. Direct biblical references, to be sure, are pinned down chapter and verse (correctly, in the cases I spot-checked). But, in "How it Feels to be Colored Me," Zora Neale Hurston says,

> I feel most colored when I am thrown against a sharp white background. For instance at Barnard. "Beside the waters of the Hudson" I feel my race. Among the thousand white persons, I am a dark rock surged upon, and overswept, but through it all, I remain myself. When covered by the waters, I am; and the ebb but reveals me again. (1651)

The note here says that Barnard is an "American women's college in New York City, near the Hudson River," which is okay, if not illuminating, but proceeds to instruct us, in parentheses, to "cf. 'by the waters of Zion.' " Hurston's biblical cadences had me cf-ing nicely on my own, thank you, though to the waters of *Babylon.* Mount Zion, home; waters of Babylon, exile. Got it? And not just in the Psalms, but in dozens and perhaps hundreds of musical settings of the text, from Nicholas Gombert's Renaissance motet to the reggae version of the traditional hymn that is used in the film *The*

Harder They Come. Students might even know one of those settings and make the connection, though not if they're told "cf. *Zion.*"

Paley has her Dennis swear "by the birdseed of St. Francis." Gilbert and Gubar Nortonize his wit by informing us that the reference is to "St. Francis of Assisi (1182?–1226), traditionally depicted feeding birds." That sure would be a surprise to Giotto and the gang, with their representations of St. Francis *preaching* to the birds! Dennis is making a little joke, but I'm afraid the editors of *NALW* are in deadly earnest. After this, would it surprise you very much to learn that the Moravian brotherhood, to which H. D.'s mother belonged, was not particularly "noted for its mysticism" as claimed on page 1458? Or that the editors make the vulgar error confusing the Immaculate Conception with the Virgin Birth (2260)?

For aspects of foreign cultures improperly explained, there is the note on Lucrezia Borgia, said to be the "cruel-eyed" woman in a Giorgione portrait that figures in George Eliot's "The Lifted Veil" (777). The footnote reads: "Lucrezia Borgia (1480–1519), daughter of a family of Italian nobles, was reputed to be vicious and wanton in her treatment of others." It goes on to tell us that Giorgione was an Italian painter and to supply the dates of his birth and death. For someone who has never seen a Giorgione and probably cannot imagine a Venetian Renaissance portrait, that line is what I would call pseudo-information, that is, not wrong, but also not useful. The ubiquity of such information in the Norton anthologies is a larger question to which I shall be returning. But, as long as there is to be a note on Lucrezia Borgia, would it not have been worthwhile to learn more about her? (E.g., that her family was not precisely noble—ecclesiastical arrivistes, nor precisely Italian—recent Spanish origin; that her father was the Pope; that the *family* was noted for cruelty in political and personal dealings, between which it often failed to discriminate to a nicety; that poisoning was its popularly attributed means of handling enemies; that Lucrezia's first couple of husbands died under highly questionable circumstances; and that her degree of complicity in their murders has never been determined.) Maybe all this explains why Lucrezia Borgia is mentioned.

To move into our own century, Zora Neale Hurston's essay speaks not only of exile, but of personal pride:

> When I set my hat at a certain angle and saunter down Seventh Avenue, Harlem City, feeling as snooty as the lions in front of the Forty-Second Street Library. . . . [s]o far as my feelings are concerned, Peggy Hopkins Joyce on the Boule Mich with her gorgeous raiment, stately carriage, knees knocking together in a most aristocratic manner, has nothing on me. (1652)

Again, the reader gets the point of this without necessarily knowing that Peggy Hopkins Joyce was an "American beauty and fashion-setter of the twenties," but there is certainly nothing wrong with having the reference explained. (Though it would also be nice if it were not taken for granted that "American beauty" means *white* American beauty unless otherwise qualified. If the note had been on that other twenties beauty and Parisian fashion-setter, Josephine Baker, the word "black" would certainly have appeared.) The *factual* problem, however, is with "Boule Mich," which the note goes on to define as "the Boulevard Saint-Michel, a fashionable street in Paris." The Boul' Mich may indeed be more chic than Telegraph Avenue, Berkeley, or Mass Ave., Cambridge, but its social and cultural significance as main drag of the student quarter is precisely comparable to that of these other thoroughfares. And Paris, unlike the aforenamed university towns, is a city that decidedly knows from fashionable streets! The original error is evidently Hurston's, but her simile works notwithstanding. The reader does not stop to think that Peggy Hopkins Joyce possibly never set foot on the Boul' Mich or that Hurston herself would have felt considerably more at home there. Only the gratuitous editorial misinformation really jars.

It does not lead us actually astray, however, unlike a note on Sylvia Plath's astonishing poem, "The Swarm." Plath says:

It is you the knives are out for
At Waterloo, Waterloo, Napoleon,
The hump of Elba on your short back . . . (2204)

Reference is made at this point to "Napoleon Bonaparte (1769–
1821) . . . France's emperor and military leader until his defeat by
the British at the battle of Waterloo in 1815 . . . [who] spent his
last days on the island of Elba, off the western coast of Italy." Holy
St. Helena, I didn't know that! I thought Elba was the site of Napoleon's exile in 1814–15, from which he returned to regroup his
Grand Army for what turned out to be the ultimate defeat at
Waterloo. I thus read Plath's later lines,

The white busts of marshals, admirals, generals
Worming themselves into niches . . . (2205)

very differently from the way I would if Elba had, in fact, been the
place of final exile.

Are the notes as systematically in error when it comes to alternative lifestyles? The evidence is rather thinner. The speaker in
Diane Wakoski's "My Trouble" complains that she has "the spirit
of Gertrude Stein/but the personality of Alice B. Toklas." Being a
Toklas type means that

all I can do
is embroider Picasso's drawings
and bake hashish fudge. (2275)

The note tells us that Stein early championed Picasso's work and,
of course, gives us Picasso's dates and nationality. It does not explain that Toklas made a couple of needlepoint chair covers (now
in Yale's Beinecke Library) from his designs, leaving that reference
unnecessarily opaque. It does, however, state that hashish fudge
was "allegedly a party delicacy served by Toklas." Just who alleges
this? The recipe for hashish fudge appears in *The Alice B. Toklas
Cookbook* as a contribution from the painter Brion Gysin. Toklas al-

ways maintained that she had not known what *Cannabis sativa* was, never actually tried the recipe herself, and definitely did not relish the subsequent scandal when the book appeared.[1] Once more, the metaphor works when Wakoski uses it, but the note codifies something that is contrary to fact.

In Alice Walker's "Everyday Use," Wangero (formerly Dee) returns home, saying "Wa-su-zo-Tean-o!" The note tells us this is a "Muslim greeting." Her male companion follows up more formally with "Asalamalakim, my mother and sister!" (2369–70). This, we are informed, is an "African dialect greeting." Not only are the labels reversed, but the notes provide *no further information whatsoever* as to what Dee-Wangero and the man her mother calls "Hakim-a-barber" are into. (Are we to conclude that their behavior is *just* ridiculous?) Hence, the reader learns nothing about the "beef-cattle peoples down the road," nor the range of black resistance in its various cultural styles. Students might even miss the significance of the narrator-mother's remark about her neighbors: "When the white folks poisoned some of the herd the men stayed up all night with rifles in their hands. I walked a mile and a half just to see the sight" (2371).

But then, the notes do tend to be gun-shy when it comes to issues that smack of radical politics. Adrienne Rich ("When We Dead Awaken") gives the editors another chance at the Bay of Pigs, including it in a list with "the sit-ins and marches in the South . . . [and] the early antiwar movement" (2053). This time, we are told that the Bay of Pigs refers to the "site of a failed American invasion of Cuba, intended to overthrow the Castro regime." No clue as to what Rich means when she puts it on her list and says that, in contrast to the masculine academy, with its "expert and fluent answers," she "needed to think for myself—about pacifism and dissent and violence, about poetry and society, and about my own relationship to all these things."

The official Gilbert and Gubar definition of "scabs" comes somewhat closer to the truth. Carolyn Kizer's "Pro Femina," excerpted in *NALW*, refers to a time "when too many girls were scabs to their stricken sisterhood" (1974). And "scabs," we are told, are "laborers who go back to work before a strike has ended." Just as Dante's hell does have seven circles, since it has nine all together, some scabs return to the job early, while some may never have gone on strike in the first place, and others may be outsiders hired once the strike is called. These different ways in which solidarity may be absent reflect the reason for Kizer's choice of metaphor. Edna St. Vincent Millay was involved in the case of Sacco and Vanzetti, who were not "alleged anarchists" as Gilbert and Gubar tell us on page 1554, but professed and unashamed anarchists who were alleged murderers. It depends on which term one considers pejorative, I guess.

Can you take some more, perhaps some miscellaneous ones? Well, Rebecca West's Jacobite fugitives hiding on the moors were followers not of James II (1595), but of his pretender-grandson, Bonnie Prince Charlie, and were defeated with him at Culloden. Lorain, Ohio, where Toni Morrison grew up and where she situates much of her fiction, has a population of 78,000; if it is not a major metropolis, it is also not a "small town" (2067). The grocers and horse dealers of *Middlemarch* certainly belong to a different social class from landowners, clergymen, bankers, or doctors. But neither George Eliot nor, one would think, anybody else—with two collaborating exceptions—would call these petty bourgeois *working* class (761). Court shoes are not for the tennis court (2235), but—being what are also called "pumps"—are presumably for the royal one. *Mais oui* and *mais non* do not mean "but yes" and "but no," as they are made to whenever these notes are called upon to translate them, because we don't *say* "but yes" and "but no" in English; we say, "why yes," "of course not," "fer-sure," and so on, depending on context.

It is not only in such odd translations that a certain tin ear for English usage is apparent in these head- and footnotes. Sylvia Plath manifested "an early precocity" (2193). Her late precocity apparently never got a chance to bloom. Maggie Tulliver's mother not only favored her son, but also preferred her "monographed linen" to her daughter (759). Surely someone could *write* a monograph on Mrs. Tulliver and her household linen but not *on* the fabric itself. Immigrants on Ellis Island were put through "lengthy customs [not immigration?] procedures" (1921). And so, unfortunately, on and on. I was unavoidably reminded of Mark Twain's observation that:

> When a person has a poor ear for music he will flat and sharp right along without knowing it. He keeps near the tune, but it is *not* the tune. When a person has a poor ear for words, the result is a literary flatting and sharping; you perceive what he is intending to say, but you also perceive that he doesn't *say* it.[2]

But can it be Gilbert and Gubar, whose prose, several or collaborative, is normally so precise and graceful, who earn Twain's epithet? Can Sandra Gilbert, an accomplished poet, actually be showing her "poor ear for words"? We have to assume that these two distinguished critics still know a monograph from a monogram and have not lost their grip, having rather loosened their hold on the enormous editorial process involved in a project like *NALW*.

Yet the responsibility, as well as the credit, is ultimately theirs. That is why it seems to me necessary to place two incommensurable quantities in some sort of balance: on the one side, the sheer joy of this big fat collection; on the other, the wrongheadedness of so very much of the interpretive apparatus. What, in short, is one to make of an anthology addressed to undergraduates (and, from certain points of view, ideally suited to that audience) that is chock-full of the kinds of errors teachers despair to find in undergraduate papers?

The problem, I believe, comes down to the view of literary education represented by the Norton series and the particular difficulties created by attempted Nortonization of a female tradition. Norton anthologies tend to be a non-elite packaging of elite content. They serve, that is, to introduce the accepted canon of British or American or "world" literature to an audience presumed to be largely unfamiliar with its contours. It is likely to be an audience encountering the canon as part of core-curriculum or general education requirements, for whom this introduction may well stand as a conclusion. The traditional "gentleman's education," with its emphasis on the literary classics and its leisured approach to the text, is here reduced to minimalism, if not to absurdity. It is my impression that the less "gentlemanly" the institution, in terms of intellectual tradition and student origins, the more likely it is to rely on Norton anthologies in the apposite courses—that is, they are used extensively by students who are the first generation of their families to attend college. The Nortons thus play a part in what one critic of the massification (as opposed to democratization) of higher education calls its "fast food" dimension.

Within the profession, complaints about the anthologies themselves are not always distinguishable from complaints about the kind of course for which they are assigned and even about the students to whom such courses are addressed. Those focusing on the collections themselves argue that a Norton anthology does not simply present the established canon, but further codifies it. The observable result has been the absence or under-representation of non-canonical voices and forms of writing. (Whence, of course, one argument for an anthology of women's literature.) The fact that many students enrolled in the Norton courses belong to segments of the population whose voices are among those excluded from "our" literary heritage enhances the irony of the situation.

Those who teach from the anthologies—and, perhaps even more, those who have the option and choose not to—also complain about the notes. The teaching of English is carried on, after all, by people who like to read a page of poetry that does *not* bristle with superscripts, and many of us want to communicate a feeling for the intact text. English professors also tend to be compulsive readers, so they are the people least able to ignore the notes to which the superscripts refer. Students may need more help than professors do, but their instructors often wonder if they need precisely the amount and kind of help represented by these pseudo-informative notes. To my mind, they create the impression that literature is a welter of esoteric, essentially self-referential remarks, interpretation of which is not unlike a game of Trivial Pursuit.

But they (the "they" who loom so large in discussions about the anthologies) don't "get" the references without help, and a lot of passages really are opaque for those who don't. Still I wonder how far knowing (say) that Michelangelo was an Italian artist who lived between certain dates will take one in understanding "The Love Song of J. Alfred Prufrock". And does one come away from a semester or a year of such information any better educated about either the particulars themselves or the literature they are meant to illuminate? I should add, however, that, although Norton notes as a genre are widely considered pedantic and (yet) oversimplified, often beside the point, I have never heard any complaints that they are inaccurate. Michelangelo is not likely to be identified in these notes as a German Expressionist painter who was T. S. Eliot's contemporary.

The Norton Anthology of Literature by Women follows the format associated with this publisher's offerings in British and American literature. In their preface, Gilbert and Gubar declare that their collection is "designed to serve as a 'core-curriculum' text for the many courses in literature by women that have been developed over the past ten years" (xxvii). Whatever one's opinion of core curricula and their consequent laying on of culture, it should be evident that courses in women's literature do not normally figure among their components.[3] There are certainly institutions where such a course is one of those that fulfills a distribution requirement in literature, but none where an overview of the female tradition or contribution is considered a necessary part of "every educated person's" cultural baggage. Courses in literature by women may be introductory in that the students who take them, whether on an elective or a "forced choice" basis, are frequently unfamiliar with the literary tradition and the apparatus of criticism. But the course is still fundamentally different from what is usually understood by "core curriculum."

More to the point, there *is* no "core curriculum" in women's literature. Whereas the other Norton anthologies present a recognized version of a given national or international literature, Gilbert and Gubar compiled this collection as part of the still-controversial assertion that there is a female tradition "which, for several centuries, has coexisted with, revised and influenced male literary models" (xxvii). Since the evidence of a female tradition is still a novel and, in some quarters, hotly contested matter, there is as yet no general agreement about what comprises it. The question therefore is whether or not literature by women is *ready* for the designation of its canon and, if a premature (and, to some, never acceptable) attempt is to be made, on what basis the contents are to be selected.

Feminist scholars have been highly visible among those who have challenged the traditional canon, the curriculum based upon it, and the textbooks serving that curriculum.[4] If many white feminists began by noticing that the voices of women could be heard only faintly in such compendia, we soon observed that writers of color and those reflecting working-class experience were also conspicuous by their absence. There was an (at least apparent) connection, then, between social power and cultural dominance. But defenders of the curricular status quo did not have to justify the existing social arrangements in order to defend their syllabi and anthologies. They tended, rather, to invoke literary standards, criteria of excellence by whose lights the canon was alleged to have been established and in accordance with which it has been maintained. If there were not very many women writers represented, it was because there have not been very many good ones. Issues of gender, race, and class tended in this way to be excluded from a discourse devoted to cultural traditions in a culture where those issues, in fact, loom very large.

Gilbert and Gubar cannot fall back on the "literary standards" argument in its purest form, because the very creation of an anthology of literature by women invokes the category of gender. It thereby not only opens the way to questions about *which* women are meant—entailing questions about race and class—but also about the word "literature"—entailing questions about genre, style, and "standards." I say the anthology raises such questions, but it also, by and large, ignores them. From its subtitle on, *NALW* is presented as "the" tradition of literature by Anglophone women, producing the implication of an unchallenged (indeed, unassailable) canon, parallel in many ways to the other canon, with which, indeed, it may overlap.

There is, admittedly, a certain polemical value in this very refusal of polemic. The editors themselves do not have to waste time defending the idea of a female tradition or the quality of its constituent texts. Implicitly, all they have to do is get on with the job. And the rest of us have a formidable new weapon to brandish in those bodies where curricular matters are determined. (I mean, of course, a rhetorical weapon, but I may not be the only one who has also been tempted to throw the thing at a recalcitrant colleague; it is a nice weight for the purpose and, properly aimed, would knock the wind out of anyone's arguments.) It is here that the blandness and respectability of the Norton label have their greatest appeal.

But the collection is intended, after all, for the classroom, not the committee room. So the question is whether the "many courses in literature by women that have developed over the past ten years" (and why ten? a decade before this book was published, a number of us were already veterans) *ought* to be presenting that literature in the Norton format. Is it right—in all the factual and ethical connotations of that word—to create the impression that there is a single, recognized tradition of women's writing? Or that this tradition offers no challenge to the aesthetic standards derived from the male-dominated canon? Or that the proportion of included writers who are not white, not at least middle class, not Anglo-American is the generally agreed upon and correct one?

At the present stage of feminist scholarship, is it right to present students with capsule histories, complete with discussions of the status of women and of women's writing in each period, without any indication of where this information comes from and how they could read further themselves? These historical introductions contain a great deal of controversial material, starting with the demarcation of non-traditional periods, but most of the controversy is not explicitly acknowledged. If the "facts" presented are incomplete or susceptible of more than one interpretation, they are nonetheless on a higher intellectual level than the notes. What the introductory essays and the notes have in common is a way of looking at knowledge that does not help students learn to think—at all, much less critically—about crucial issues.

As for those notes, do we really want students to perceive "the" women's tradition as being, like the other Norton literary traditions, mere patterns of euphonious esoterica? Must Norton notes be the price we pay for the anthology's existence? If so, what are we to think when these are not just your usual dumb notes, but passkeys to vast realms of factual error? What difference does it make if someone who is never going to read Dante's *Inferno* is permanently misinformed about how many circles it contains? Very little, unless she misses the question on an old-fashioned TV quiz show and sues for educational malpractice. The real malpractice lies in the assumption that she never will read a poem that does not figure in the syllabus, and that it is no part of an educator's job to stimulate her interest in doing so.

A number of the misstated facts are similarly anodyne in appearance, at least taken individually. In the aggregate, they provide a notably bum steer about belief systems, both orthodox and radical, cultural styles, the texture of other societies—all of which leads to an impoverishment of life.[5] Can we assume with equanimity that those students who will never read Dante will also never see Paris, find the poetry in an old hymn, challenge the hegemony of supermarkets, or walk a picket line, daring the scabs to cross? And should an educator, a *feminist* educator, be content to have it so? My own belief is that women's studies is a classier act than that.

NOTES

1. See *The Alice B. Toklas Cookbook* itself (New York: Harper, 1954); *Staying On Alone: Letters of Alice B. Toklas*, ed. Edward Burns (New York: Liveright, 1973); and the account in Linda Simon, *The Biography of Alice B. Toklas* (New York: Doubleday, 1977). Simon summarizes Toklas's response this way: "To think that she and Gertrude had been indulging in hashish all these years and to think that the resulting state of mind might account for Gertrude's writing infuriated her" (270).

2. Mark Twain, "Fenimore Cooper's Literary Offenses" (1895), in *American Literary Essays*, ed. Lewis Leary (New York: Crowell, 1960), p. 87.

3. The "laying on of culture" is a phrase that I have not used or even heard in a number of years, which is not to say that there is less of it going around. The phrase originated in New Left analysis of the class nature of higher education, specifically in the work of John McDermott, and is intended to charac-

terize the role and attitude post-secondary educators often assume vis-à-vis their working-class students.

4. For an overview of this issue, see my article, "Treason Our Text: Feminist Challenges to the Literary Canon," pp. 1–22 and its companion piece, "Their Canon, Our Arsenal," pp. 23–37. A number of Paul Lauter's articles deal specifically with the results of the canon-formation process as reflected in textbook anthologies.

5. It should be pointed out that my survey of errors is by no means exhaustive. Another reader, with other preoccupations and other miscellaneous information, might come up with a different list of perhaps equal length.

I wanted to update "Is There Class in This Text?" for the present collection, but rapidly figured out that it couldn't be done. An additional short essay, which I wrote in early May 1996, was required. Once I began this one, I discovered, much to my surprise, that I was able to recapture at least some of the seriousness and some of the fun of "Is There Class . . . ?"

THE QUEENS' NECKLACE

I figure if it was good enough for Dumas, *père*, it's good enough for me. The title, that is. Once it became apparent that developments in the decade since I reviewed *The Norton Anthology of Literature by Women* ("Is There Class in This Text?" pp. 49–66) called for more than a follow-up footnote, I gave the brief essay I envisaged—this one—the working title "Ten Years After." It didn't ring true, though, because, as a child following the adventures of the Three Musketeers through the sequel, I read and reread *Twenty Years After*. (I was an equal-opportunity book-devourer, in whose imagination Athos, Porthos, Aramis, and D'Artagnan were the boon companions of Meg, Jo, Beth, and Amy).

So "Ten Years After" just sounded funny.[1] In any event, I had another youthful Dumas memory to pay homage to, *The Queen's Necklace*, set 160 years after D'Artagnan dashed into Paris on that buttercup-colored nag. The ear, I felt, would not detect my displacement of the apostrophe the way it did the false note of "Ten Years After." The *NALW*, after all, is certainly one of the crown jewels that signal its editors' status in the realm of feminist criticism. And, of course, the thing about the queen's necklace is that the real one was the object of intrigues, plots, and counterplots. It didn't get to occupy its rightful place on the queen's throat, which, as Wayne Koestenbaum's title reminds us, is that of a diva, a prima donna. In feminist criticism, moreover, the Gilbert and Gubar collaboration is as familiar an icon as the musketeers who were "all for one and one for all." And for anyone who remembers that the senior Alexandre Dumas ran what was arguably the biggest writing factory in Europe, hiring countless assistants who shared neither profit, credit, nor blame for the *oeuvre* he signed, the fact will, perhaps, go some way toward elucidating the curious editorial lapses to which my review of the *NALW* called attention.

This book is scheduled to go to press shortly before the appearance of the second edition of the *NALW*. Having commented on a number of erroneous details in the first edition, I think it would be unfair and inappropriate to form my judgment of the revision on the basis of the uncorrected proofs that may be available at this time. The new subtitle—*Traditions in English* in lieu of the definite article and a single tradition—suggests welcome changes in approach, so it may be that the criticisms recorded in this essay no longer apply. But, in that case, it is all the more important to recall the critical history that was instrumental in bringing those changes into being and not act as if they are a product of natural evolution.

Most of the negative responses evoked by *The Norton Anthology of Literature by Women* came from outside the academy, chiefly from reviewers and journalists who rejected and sneered at gender as a category of literary description or analysis. Novelist Gail Godwin's diatribe in *The New York Times Book Review* also bore the unmistakable stamp of the competitor—an athlete, say—who, having failed to make the cut, declared that there was no rationale for the existence of the team. The collection's generally favorable reception among feminist critics reflects a more thoughtful, as well as a more sympathetic approach. (I am thinking particularly of Lee Edwards's piece in *Women's Review of Books* [June, 1986] and Sandra Zagarell's essay, which was paired with mine in *Tulsa Studies*.)

But, beyond the genuine appreciation (one for all), there was also a sense that feminist criticism had closed ranks (all for one) against the know-nothing assault from the know-it-alls who were so ready to dismiss our field out of hand. Reported reactions to my review often reflected this professional solidarity, playing the full register from "What a nerve!" to "What nerve!"—that is, from *How dare Lillian criticize feminist colleagues when they—and, thereby, we—are under attack?* through *How dare she criticize such important and admired figures?* to *How dare she criticize such powerful ones?*

I am aware of three other sites of feminist dissatisfaction with the collection. Two of these critiques were to some extent mediated by my review. The most serious of all, however, came into being entirely independent of anything I had to say. This was the widespread and openly expressed indignation on the part of Latina feminists at the omission of Hispanic women authors from the anthology, a critique that led to an ongoing, though unorganized, boycott of the book as a classroom text. In the years since the initial publication of the *NALW*, even more readers have become familiar with the many Hispanic writers whose primary medium is standard English, as well as with others whose linguistic code-switching is a cutting-edge variation on it. Writers such as Sandra Cisneros, Lorna Dee Cervantes, Gloria Anzaldúa, Cherríe Moraga, Julia Alvarez, Christina García, Nicholasa Mohr, Ana Lydia Vega, and Rosario Ferré have achieved greater literary prominence, while Anzaldúa's theories about *mestizaje* have provided a theoretical underpinning for the bicultural female experience. Several strong anthologies foreground the traditions—always already understood as multiple—linking U.S. writers of Hispanic background or placing them in the larger context of American women writers of color.[2] These developments and the critical outcry that called attention to them may, together, be responsible for the greater inclusiveness implicit in the *NALW*'s new subtitle.

My original review was derailed from considerations of specific inclusions and exclusions by the over-arching scholarly and pedagogical issues that I thought took precedence. But it was obvious to me that African Americans are the only writers of color to receive any serious attention in the collection. Unless I've missed something, Mourning Dove and Leslie Marmon Silko are the only Native Americans in the book, Maxine Hong Kingston the only Asian American, Ama Ata Aidoo the only African, Kamala Das not just the only Indian but the only writer included from all of Anglophone Asia, and (white) Jean Rhys the only representative from the Caribbean. All the writers from the Antipodes are white descendants of immigrants from the British Isles—no Maori or aboriginal writers and no one of Asian or "other" European origin.

Now, in a literary trajectory that spans six centuries, beginning with Julian of Norwich and Margery Kempe in the 1300s and ending with Silko, who was born in 1948, it is admittedly no easy matter to determine the appropriate proportion to allot to literatures that have flourished chiefly in the latter half of the present century. But surely a book that purports to encompass the whole English-language tradition cannot be said to be doing its job if it gives such short shrift to the entire postcolonial world! As far as I know, there has been no protest on behalf of these other groups—certainly none on the scale of the Latina one. For that very reason, I shall be interested to see whether the various anthologies of literature and criticism and a new generation of reference books have brought nonblack American writers of color and world literature in English far enough into the light for them to be featured or even noticed in the new *NALW*.[3]

Two other feminist interrogations of the Norton explicitly connect to issues raised in my review. One of the earliest citations of "Is There Class in This Text?" extended my argument about the legitimacy and timeliness of declaring that it is possible to establish "the" women's tradition in English letters. In her study *Feminist Literary History*, Janet Todd, after observing that my "witty debunking" of the *NALW*'s footnotes made the anthology seem "just slightly absurd" as an enterprise, builds on my use of the word "premature" to characterize the canon-making project.[4] Todd's position is that the time is not yet ripe for construction of a female canon, because much empirical, archival, and theoretical work remains to be done. She also locates the origins of any "tradition" (the skeptical quotation marks are hers) far earlier than do Gilbert and Gubar, adding firmly that "the *Norton Anthology* is based on the assumptions of its selectors. Perhaps we need to discuss those assumptions before they are Nortonized."[5]

Tulsa Studies published only one letter in response to "Is There Class in This Text?" In that letter, Angela Ingram opens another line of questioning, one that could occur only to someone who had not boycotted the *NALW* but had actually used it in the classroom. Teaching the book had revealed an enormity even more basic than the misinformation I found in the notes. In a number of cases, the texts themselves are corrupt. Ingram pointed out that selections from Virginia Woolf and Sarah Orne Jewett end rather abruptly— because they were printed without their final paragraphs in Woolf's case and sentences in Jewett's—and that the Gilbert and Gubar version of Tillie Olsen's "Tell Me a Riddle" excises most of the first crucial passage in which the elderly grandmother cannot bear to touch the new baby. In its place, "two lines from the end of that section are appended to the next section, and the first paragraph of *that* section is then repeated."[6] As with the glaringly erroneous notes, the inaccurate texts obviously make it much harder—at times, impossible—for students or their instructors to get the reading right.

Ingram makes another version of the "one for all" argument when she points out that the slatternly scholarship, both textual and interpretive, can be used against all of us in women's studies. In a context, she argues, in which feminism continues to evoke skepticism, if not outright contempt, the "unprofessional, sloppy mess" that is this textbook places the field and its practitioners in danger of being hounded or laughed out of the academy. I couldn't read Ingram's argument without speculating about the horror beyond the one she identifies: Since no one teaches the *NALW*'s entire 2300-plus pages of text and since there is no open clearinghouse for reporting errata when they are discovered, the full extent of the textual mish mash remains unknown! In my review, I reported errors that I'd discovered in a rapid perusal of the notes, acknowledging that these had struck my eye because of my particular areas of interest and information but that readers with different preoccupations might notice mistakes that had eluded me. Similarly, Ingram records the misprints she has come across in class and, at least by implication, suggests that they are just the tip of an iceberg of untold dimensions.

It seems to me that the only appropriate response Gilbert and Gubar could have made to Ingram's discoveries would have been a red-faced "Oh my God!" Instead, their letter to *Tulsa Studies* goes on the offensive. Refusing to address the gravity of the errors Ingram identified or the consequences she claimed they might entail for all of us, they trivialize her objections by focusing on the form and the forum she chose for their presentation.[7] In a move that I'm afraid reminds me more of administrative discourse than academic interchange, they castigate Ingram for making a public announcement of her findings—to W. W. Norton's representative and the readership of *Tulsa Studies*—rather than approaching them, the two *NALW* editors, privately about their public mistakes. They also urge readers to let Norton know about such errors as they find them, so that corrections may be made from one printing to the next. I guess I can't expect Gilbert and Gubar to share my curiosity about how many textual errors there are or Ingram's feeling that those using the present version of the text need to be warned.

As they ask for readers' "help" with their enormous (not to mention lucrative) project, their sense of feminist collectivity is clearly a one-way street. Ingram's breach of the all-for-one united front is all the more heinous, they add, in that she knew one member of the pair well enough to have once requested a recommendation from her. The issue is thus cathected into either the bureaucratic or the personal dimension—or both at once—with no space for according Ingram's legitimate concerns the respect they are due. Rather, Ingram is accused of being the one to "trash" women's studies. (Is it the Red or the White Queen who says, "Off with her head"? Well, neither, of course; it's the Queen of Hearts, but you see my point.) If the penalty for writing an indignant letter to the editor of a feminist academic journal is to be read out of feminism, it's small wonder that other critical voices are muted. There are some who genuinely believe that the quality of Gilbert and Gubar's work is unassailable and others who accept their definition of uncritical feminist solidarity. Unfortunately, there are still others who are afraid to speak out for fear of retaliation.

We will have to await the second edition to learn whether my own substantive comments have been heeded or whether Napoleon is still dying on Elba and St. Francis still unoratorically feeding the birdies. As I say, the new subtitle is encouraging as regards the issue of inclusion. But neither have I entirely escaped the personal and personalized response. At the end of 1995, Gilbert and Gubar published a short play, *Masterpiece Theatre*, about the culture wars and the belligerents on both (or rather all) sides of the struggle.[8] This motley crew, which the authors' introduction compares to Matthew Arnold's ignorant armies that clash by night, includes characters named "Sandra Gilbert" and "Susan Gubar"—usually identified as SG1 and SG2—and "Lillian S. Robinson."

As is perhaps inevitable in satire, the authors position themselves above the fray and its participants—including their own alter egos with their incessant private jokes, self-castigation *for* the private jokes, and tendency to complete each other's sentences. The lofty tone is particularly annoying in the introduction, where they lay out a set of unexciting propositions that purportedly embody what "both sides fail to realize." (Well, I don't fail to realize them, damn it, and I don't think many others do, either.) *Masterpiece Theatre*'s plot revolves around a threatened and fugitive Text that SG1 and SG2, with far too little assistance (some of it from fiction writers and some from fictitious characters), ardently try to save. (Those who took Angela Ingram's revelations to heart will be interested in this belated devotion to the poor, beleaguered text.)

The character called "Lillian S. Robinson" descends *ex machina*—or at least from a commuter plane—and delivers herself of a number of anti-canonical remarks. "I'm not here to save the text," she tells a press conference. "I'm here to commit treason" (46). (This kind of in-group reference is pervasive in *Masterpiece Theatre*.) My favorite moment is where "I" say to "Jane Tompkins" (otherwise—or rather elsewhere—a real person) and Jane Marple (the invented grandniece of Agatha Christie's detective spinster), "We should get these men [William Bennett and Frank Lentricchia] out of here. Their stupid macho behavior isn't going to help anything" (51). At which SG1 and SG2, overhearing, "nod sagely."

But, a moment later, quoting my/her-self (way) out of context, "Robinson" says, "We should only really struggle to reclaim this text if it was composed by 'the previously inarticulate, the semi-literate, the consumer of popular literature' " (51). I leave it to the reader of "Canon Fathers and Myth Universe" (see especially page 84 of the present volume) to determine whether, in good faith, my remarks can possibly be construed as meaning that I value only the texts produced by those excluded groups. Meanwhile, it is in reference to this quotation that I (*think* I) get paid back for my comments on the *NALW*. At the end of the play, in lieu of notes, there is an alphabetized list of the *dramatis personae*, giving the source for any direct citations from the characters' actual works. My line is correctly ascribed to "Canon Fathers," and that passage of the article is said to appear on page 263 of Ralph Cohen's collection *The Future of Literary Theory*. In fact, what's on that page is part of an essay, also quoted in *Masterpiece Theatre*, by Gerald Graff, while no work of mine is published in *The Future of Literary Theory*.[9]

I have no idea if this was intentional. But perhaps it's not too far-fetched to wonder whether, in order to memorialize and embody the position that all I was doing in "Is There Class in This Text?" was splitting hairs over footnotes, I am condemned forever—or for as much of forever as an ephemeral piece of satire endures—to incarceration *in the wrong footnote!* That'll show me! Well, maybe, but what I hope to be shown, instead, is a revised and responsible second edition of *The Norton Anthology of Literature by Women*. Really.

NOTES

1. Yes, I know there's a band called Ten Years After. They played at Woodstock.

2. See, for example, for Latinas: *Cuentos: Stories by Latinas*, ed. Alma Gómez, Cherríe Moraga, and Mariana Romo-Camona (New York: Kitchen Table Women of Color Press, 1983), *Chicana Creativity and Criticism*, ed. María Herrera-Sobek and Helena María Viramontes (Houston: Arte Publico, 1986), *Reclaiming Medusa: Short Stories by Contemporary Puerto Rican Women*, ed. Diana Velez (San Francisco: Spinsters/Aunt Lute, 1988), *Breaking Boundaries: Latina Writings and Critical Readings*, ed. Asunción Horno-Delgado, et al. (Amherst: University of Massachusetts Press, 1989); for Native Americans: *In the Fire of Time: The Voice of Native American Women* (New York: Dutton, 1977), *That's What She Said: Contemporary Poetry and Fiction by Native American Women*, ed. Rayna Green (Bloomington: Indiana University Press, 1984), *Spider Woman's Grand-daughters: Traditional Tales and Contemporary Writing by Native American Women*, ed. Paula Gunn Allen (Boston: Beacon Press, 1989); for Asian Americans: *Making Waves: An Anthology of Writing by and about Asian American Women*, ed. Asian Women United of California (Boston: Beacon Press, 1989), *The Forbidden Stitch: An Asian American Women's Anthology*, ed. Shirley Geok-lin Lim and Hayumi Tsutakawa (Corvallis, OR: Calyx, 1992), *The Politics of Life: Four Plays by Asian American Women*, ed. Velina Hasu Houston (Philadelphia: Temple University Press, 1992), *Unbroken Thread: An Anthology of Plays by Asian American Women*, ed. Roberta Uno (Amherst: University of Massachusetts Press, 1993); for works with an over-arching women-of-color perspective: *This Bridge Called My Back: Writing by Radical Women of Color*, ed. Gloria Anzaldúa and Cherríe Moraga (Boston: Persephone, 1981), *Haciendo Caras/Making Face, Making Soul*, ed. Gloria Anzaldúa (San Francisco: Spinsters/Aunt Lute, 1991); for much of the Third World: *Motherlands: Black Women's Writing from Africa, the Caribbean, and South Asia*, ed. Shusheila Nasta (New Brunswick, NJ: Rutgers University Press, 1992); for Africa: *Unwinding Threads: Writing by Women in Africa* (London: Heinemann, 1983), *The Heinemann Book of African Women's Writing*, ed. Charlotte H. Bruner (London: Heinemann, 1993), *The Heinemann Book of African Women's Poetry*, ed. Stella and Frank Chipasula (London: Heinemann, 1995); for West Indian writers: *Watchers and Seekers: Creative Writing by Black Women*, ed. Rhonda Cobham and Merle Collins (New York: Peter Bedrick, 1987), *Creation Fire: A CAFRA Anthology of Women's Poetry*, ed. Ramabai Espinet (Toronto: CAFRA/Sister Vision Press, 1991); for Australian "others": *Beyond the Echo: Multicultural Women's Writing*, ed. Sneja Gunew and Jan Mahyuddin (St. Lucia: University of Queensland Press, 1988).

3. See the critical essays in the two Chicana collections cited above; for criticism on Native Americans, see: *Studies in American Indian Literature: Critical Essays and Course Designs*, ed. Paula Gunn Allen (New York: Modern Language Association, 1983), *Recovering the Word: Essays in Native American Literature*, ed. Brian Swann and Arnold Krupat (Berkeley: University of California Press, 1987), *New Voices in Native American Literary Criticism*, ed. Arnold Krupat (Washington, D.C.: Smithsonian Institution Press, 1993); on Asian Americans: *Reading the Literature of Asian America*, ed. Shirley Geok-lin Lim and Amy Ling (Philadelphia: Temple University Press, 1992); on Africans: *Ngambika: Studies*

of Women in African Literature, ed. Carole Boyce Davies and Anne Adams Graves (Trenton: Africa World, 1986), *Women in African Literature Today*, ed. Eldred Durosini Jones, et al. (Trenton, NJ: Africa World, 1987); for West Indians: *Out of the Kumbla: Caribbean Women and Literature*, ed. Carole Boyce Davies and Elaine Savory Fido (Trenton, NJ: Africa World, 1990), *Caribbean Women Writers: Essays from the First International Conference*, ed. Selwyn R. Cudjoe (Wellesley/ Amherst: Calaloux/University of Massachusetts Press, 1990).

Useful reference collections include *The Feminist Companion to Literature in English: Women Writers from the Middle Ages to the Present*, ed. Virginia Blain, Patricia Clements, and Isobel Grundy (New Haven: Yale University Press, 1990), *The Bloomsbury Guide to Women's Literature*, ed. Claire Buck (New York: Prentice Hall, 1992), *Encyclopedia of World Literature in the 20th Century*, especially Volume 5, Supplement, ed. Steven Serafin and Walter D. Glanze (New York: Continuum, 1993). Recently added to this list are the four volumes of my own reference collection, *Modern Women Writers*, ed. Lillian S. Robinson, 4 volumes (New York: Continuum, 1996).

4. Janet Todd, *Feminist Literary History* (New York: Routledge, 1988), pp. 47–48. See also Florence Howe's introduction to her collection *Tradition and the Talents of Women* (Urbana: University of Illinois Press, 1991), where she states that the *NALW* established, "at least for the 1980s, a canon of women writers that nevertheless cannot help failing to satisfy" (14).

5. Ibid., p. 48.

6. Angela Ingram, Letter to the Editor, *Tulsa Studies in Women's Literature*, 6:2 (1987), 373–74.

7. Sandra M. Gilbert and Susan Gubar, Letter to the Editor, *Tulsa Studies in Women's Literature*, 7:1 (1988), 159.

8. Sandra M. Gilbert and Susan Gubar, *Masterpiece Theatre: An Academic Melodrama* (New Brunswick, NJ: Rutgers University Press, 1995).

9. You could look it up: *The Future of Literary Theory*, ed. Ralph Cohen (New York: Routledge, 1989).

I wrote this piece to present during a March 1986 campus interview for a job chairing a Comparative Literature Program. The post
went to someone else. Later that year, unemployed, I gave it as a
guest lecture at a university where I was told an opening in feminist criticism might be redesigned to fit me. It wasn't. Since I was
still recuperating from a bout of pneumonia and way over deadline
for the *New Literary History* Symposium I'd agreed to contribute to,
I sent in "Canon Fathers" in lieu of my comments. Editor Ralph
Cohen wisely observed that my contribution was not a response to
Ellen Messer-Davidow's "The Philosophical Bases of Feminist Literary Criticism" and offered to publish it, instead, with several other
articles that were to precede the symposium in the same special issue on "Feminist Directions" (Volume 19, 1987–88). It has been reprinted in two collections, once with a horrible misprint where the
elephant-seals paragraph comes up twice—in the place where it belongs, but also, incongruously, a couple of pages earlier.

CANON FATHERS AND MYTH UNIVERSE

In the subtext of these remarks are two questions that, together, constitute the pretext for what follows. The first of these questions is that of the reader who asks, *What the hell does that title mean, anyway: Canon Fathers and Myth Universe?* Well, it refers to the generally patriarchal literary canon, the literally patriarchal biblical one that is the source of the canon metaphor, the Fathers of the Church, whose patristic writings include the bases of canon law, the Anglican cathedral clergy, whose title is "canon" and who may be addressed as "Father," and, of course, the military imagination, with its fecund visions of can(n)on fodder. And then there are the notions of a universal myth, the *dominant* myth of a human universal that turns out to be male, and the sexist international competition for Miss Universe. My title is at once the portmanteau that contains all that conceptual baggage and the background upon which the essay itself is projected.

The other question in my sub- and pre-text is one that I have been asking myself with increasing insistence whenever I accept an invitation to give a guest lecture under the aegis of a Department of English or Comparative Literature. Crudely expressed (which is exactly how it *is* expressed in the depths of my consciousness), my question goes: *Shall I choose a subject in feminist criticism or in "regular" criticism?*

This is a genuine question. On the one hand, my reputation and intellectual identity have both been informed by my work as a feminist critic. But the invitation is frequently at the instance of a search committee, as part of the hiring process. As a professional who is not gainfully employed, ought I not show that I can do regular criticism too? So the question is heartfelt and authentic. Yet it horrifies me. For criticism should not be served, like coffee, in "regular" and "variant" versions. In fact, though, depending on the region of this country in which you order it, "regular" coffee is interpreted as meaning that the cream has been added or, conversely, that it has not. (Regular, that is, is the opposite of both black and white—depending on where you stand.) Surely, I have been telling myself, I can construct an argument to show why, at this time, the proper project of "regular" criticism is the one with the feminism *in* it.

In the context in which it originated, my project was clearly something of a peace initiative, an attempt to demonstrate that feminist criticism is not fundamentally different from (and hence in no way a threat to) dominant critical modalities. In its evolution, however, that irenic effort asserted its true identity, coming to resemble a declaration of permanent difference, if not precisely of war, more than the patching-over I intended. For I find that, despite the most pacific intentions, I am still asking to what extent a feminist perspective necessarily challenges all the previous assumptions and conclusions of the critical tradition.

It is on this basis that I inaugurated the Visiting Humanities Chair I occupied at Albright College, a few years ago, by delivering a lecture entitled "Why Studying Women Means Studying Everything." The anecdotes with which I began that lecture, although they are drawn from other fields, have a special pertinence to the study of literature. Despite that global title, these anecdotes deal modestly enough with my nephew Ian and the elephant seals. They are two distinct stories, but both have their ramifications, and those ramifications turn out to touch each other at a number of points.

When Ian was a teenager, I was invited from Paris to New York for a series of interviews and took advantage of that time for several marathon work sessions with my collaborators on the book *Feminist Scholarship: Kindling in the Groves of Academe.*[1] I was accompanied on my travels by my infant son, who acquired three new teeth in the two weeks we spent in America. As you can imagine, I was much in need of and very grateful for the heroic hours of babysitting provided by Ian and his younger brother. In order to help me in this way, Ian had to refuse requests for his services from his regular clients. He expatiated to me on the relative thickness of blood and water. Then, referring to the neighbor he'd just turned down for the second or third time that week, he added, "Besides, your work is more important than hers. She's just writing some book about women in the French Revolution." Reluctant as I would have been to lose or even share my sitter, I had to know: Why was he so prepared to dismiss this work? "Well," he explained, "it can't be very important. I mean, *I* never heard of any women in the French Revolution!"[2] In the fine tradition of child psychology represented by Ring Lardner's line " 'Shut up,' I explained," *I* explained at the top of my lungs that it was precisely to prevent fourteen-year-old smart asses from being so sure that women were absent from the great events of history that such intellectual work *was* important. This story turns out to have a range of applications to literary study, and I shall be discussing some of them shortly.

First, however, the elephant seals. An elephant seal, which I once heard a lecturer describe as looking, in motion, like a cross between a walrus and a waterbed, belongs to a species of belatedly protected wildlife that lives in the Pacific Ocean. Every January, they all come up to Año Nuevo Beach near Santa Cruz, California, and to an island just off its shore, to mate. Each year, thousands of human visitors descend on Año Nuevo in a spirit of learned voyeurism to find out about the elephant seals and their environment. The actual mating takes place on the island, so it is something of an exaggeration to say, as people tend to, "We're going to see (or *watch*) the elephant seals mate." What you do see are seals, asleep, tending their young, or galumphing about, and sometimes interacting with one another. To interpret this set of observations and particularly the interactions, there is an army of volunteer docents, as well as a mass of posters, bulletin boards, and fliers. What emerges from the surfeit of natural history is a picture of male elephant seals fighting it out for dominance over one another in order to be able to control territory and hence to control females. The largest, most aggressive, and dominant males, we are told, win big harems for the mating season, those who are less so get less space and fewer females in the harem, and the adolescents—old enough to mate but not large enough to compete—join the pups and the wimps in hanging out on the beach. Elephant seal behavior that may appear random, playful, or at least neutral to the lay observer is invariably characterized in terms of this rigid lexicon of dominance, hierarchy, territory, and harems.[3]

Now, I have been to see the elephant seals a number of times, and my irritation was at first inflamed by the racist description of the Indians who used to inhabit that section of the coast, a racism presented in the same blandly factual tone as the ecology lecture. (They "disappeared," we were told, but their mysterious evanescence was no great loss, for they were not particularly "interesting" Indians. Lacking a sense of history, it seems, they "had no culture" worth speaking of!) It was this rhetoric that made me compare what was said and written, which is to say *interpreted*, about the elephant seals—as text, if you will—with what could actually be observed. I concluded that all that really can be stated, more humbly but far more honestly, about the elephant seals is that they do come back to Año Nuevo to mate and that not much is really understood about their behavior, their motives, or their community. Perhaps one could add that male elephant seals seem to feel a need for a lot of space around them at mating time and that females prefer to be closer together at that time, as well as at the subsequent birthing of the pups. That is absolutely all we know, and the rest is projecting an oppressive anthropomorphic scenario on those poor creatures just trying to go about the business of reproducing their species.

Within the general framework of canon formation, re-formation, and reformation consequent upon the emergence of feminist criticism, I take the exemplary tale about my nephew and the revolutionary Frenchwomen to embody certain truths about the recovery of women's role in *literary* history. The elephant seals I take as emblematic of the problems—but also the opportunities—encountered when we bring women's reclaimed role into relation with the literary tradition as it has hitherto been perceived.

If you've never heard of any women in the French Revolution, this is a commentary on historical scholarship and even on historians, not on women in the French Revolution. That, of course, is the gist of what I yelled at my nephew. And so, too, in literary studies, where an impressive labor of intellectual reappropriation has begun to document the existence of a continuous tradition of women's writing in English, as well as in a number of other European literatures, a tradition extending well back into the centuries before the Industrial Revolution. Feminist scholarship has also challenged canonical definitions of literature itself by exploring women's private writings—letters, journals, personal memoirs—as literary texts. And it has sought access to mass female experience by considering popular genres produced by women for the female audience as a possible component of the newly acknowledged entity "women's literature." This inclusiveness, where there was once only a brief but oft-rehearsed litany of great names, has also meant a slow opening of the emerging female tradition to the voices of women of color, lesbians who write from and of that experience, and women writing out of the (literal) history of colonization and its aftermath.

But what about "the" canon, the regular canon, so to speak? How, to use my analogy from the study of history, do we fit the recently uncovered activities of women into the old story of the French Revolution? There are two quite different approaches to this question. The first is simply to add the new information about what women did to the body of information already in our possession. The second is to raise a more thoroughgoing question: How does what we have learned about the role of women *change* what we know or believe we know about the French Revolution in general? To situate it in the literary context: How does the newly uncovered material by seventeenth-century women affect our previous generalizations about the literature of the seventeenth century? And the answer to that question turns out to depend on essentially aesthetic considerations.

These questions, significant as they are for how we think about, say, seventeenth-century poetry, become even more crucial as we consider the various nontraditional *kinds* of texts—the diaries, the sensational or domestic novels—that are part of the women's canon. Does the act of reclamation itself imply a new aesthetic? If so, what is that new aesthetic? What are its new limits?

Similarly, once women's literature includes the writing of women of color, generalizations about "the" female imagination have to be modified accordingly. When this happens, what about "the" canon as it is confronted with the sensibility of the formerly colonized, domestic or foreign? (Here, of course, we are approaching elephant seal territory.) Certainly, one's sense of the present world-historic moment in literature—in English, but also in other national traditions—is quite different depending on the degree to which one is open to this global perspective.

As it happens, moreover, students of women's role in the actual French Revolution have brought to light a most extraordinary series of texts, the *cahiers des plaintes et doléances* written on behalf of women as women. Remarkably modern documents, insofar as they raise issues that we today would label "sexual harassment" or "the right to a career," they are also a remarkable piece of eighteenth-century history, speaking as they do *of* the condition and *in* something very like the voice of the fishwife, the flower seller, the laundress of that period.[4] Unlike the cahiers prepared by males familiar with legal forms and conventions, these documents manage to deal with issues as various as the nature of citizenship, the rights of illegitimate children, and the adulteration of laundry soap, maintaining all the while a clear focus on the connections between and among them in creating the lives of women.[5]

My own impulse would be to admit these documents as women's literature, thus making my French Revolution anecdote part of *my* critical text, rather than a metaphor stretched in a number of different directions. But when women's literature starts including the previously inarticulate, the semiliterate, the consumer of popular literature, the literature she consumes, and the writing she does on the basis of that "bad" stylistic model, it offers a challenge to "the" canon. It is a challenge to open its own frontiers not only to excluded social groups, but to the widest range of expression of those groups' experience. The result would be to see our whole past, the seventeenth and eighteenth centuries, for starters, as experienced authentically by two sexes and all classes, or our present moment as experienced by all sorts of people with very different relations to the dominant culture and the fact of dominance. And it would be to understand this seeing as a legitimate part of our activity in the world of literary interpretation, not belonging to some other mode of apprehension outside the proper boundaries of criticism.

And here we are right down on the beach with the elephant seals, trying to determine how many of the truths about our culture that we have absorbed can survive such an intellectual upheaval. The confusion starts, of course, with that word *our*, for, as Jane Flax has succinctly put it, "only recently have scholars begun to consider the possibility that there may be at least three histories in every culture—'his,' 'hers,' and 'ours.' 'His' and 'ours' are generally assumed to be equivalents."[6] What I have been doing in questioning that equivalency is to imply the existence of something very like the Outsiders' Society that Virginia Woolf unforgettably creates in *Three Guineas*. My assumption is that the logic of feminist scholarship and criticism, because they invariably bring one social category, that of gender, into relation with traditional critical categories, necessarily entails rethinking the entire literary tradition in order to place centrally into it not only an entire excluded sex—

which is an enormous enough task—but also excluded classes, races, national groups, sexual minorities, and ideological positions, as well. (I have also felt free, for the purposes of this ideal system, to ignore both the congruences *and the conflicts* between and among the various groups defined by their enforced cultural marginality.) What this means is a more truly comparative literature, one that could, in fact, comfortably be called *our* literature, rather than allowing the universe of cultural expression to remain, in the words of the Nigerian social critic Chinweizu, "the West and the rest of us."[7]

But, as I have indicated, feminist criticism can approach the traditional standards for canonicity, which are supposed to constitute "our" common aesthetic, either by demonstrating how the female tradition conforms to that aesthetic or by challenging the aesthetic itself. Similarly, in speaking of those previously excluded from elite definitions of culture, we ought to recognize where those groups both do and do not partake of "the" tradition. It is this question, both sides of it, that has impelled me to consider the myths that recur in the Western (which is to say, the white Euro-American male, high-cultural) literary tradition. I am principally concerned with them *as* part of literature, that is, not so much as archetypes as *stories* that get told over and over and whose retellings according to the imperatives of different generations depend on the long history of previous tellings.

From this point of view, as you switch perspectives from "insiders" to "outsiders," you note different priorities and preoccupations. Women writers, for instance, do not compulsively retell the history of the Trojan War and its aftermath, not even adapting the myth to fit female conditions. Indeed, in a brilliant paper at the 1984 MLA convention, Carolyn Heilbrun contrasted the literary projects of Joyce and Woolf, citing *Ulysses* as the closing off, in our century's terms, of one myth, while Woolf's work opened new mythopoeic areas for women. In a simpler vein, I find it impossible to imagine *The Odyssey au féminin* because, in the travels of any female, the sexual question looms larger and creates new difficulties of its own. Whom Does She Sleep With? becomes so central as to block out all the other questions such a myth is supposed to answer. It may be that Erica Jong has something like *The Odyssey* in mind as she serializes the adventures of Isadora Wing, particularly in her latest version, *Parachutes and Kisses*, which involves the artist's wanderings and her search for identity through reclamation of the life of the dead artist-patriarch, her grandfather. But Jong's obsessive answering and answering the Whom-Does-She-Sleep-With question obscures the rest for us, and makes all her work at least as picaresque as her intentional eighteenth-century pastiche, *Fanny*. Meanwhile, for most women writers, the Ulysses myth has proved even less useful, remaining essentially external to any central female project.

However, certain words, forms, and stories from the insiders' tradition *have* been usefully appropriated by the outsiders, and transformed in the process. When the Nigerian novelist Chinua Achebe told us in the very title of his first novel that *Things Fall Apart*, he meant things quite different from what Yeats meant in *his* colony. The use of that title signaled a simultaneous joining of the dominant tradition and an appropriation of it to different needs. The final irony in this deeply ironic novel is that it ends with the colonial District Commissioner contemplating *his* eventual text. Speaking of the central character, the last *African* voice in the novel has "ferociously" told him: "That man was one of the greatest men in Umuofia. You drove him to kill himself; and now he will be buried like a dog. . . . " Then the speaker's "voice trembled and choked his words." The administrator, by contrast, thinks that the hero's story "would make interesting reading. One could almost write a whole chapter on him. Perhaps not a whole chapter but a reasonable paragraph, at any rate. There was so much else to include, and one must be firm in cutting out details. He had already chosen the title of his book, after much thought: *The Pacification of the Primitive Tribes of the Lower Niger*."[8] Achebe ends his novel just here, but, in taking his title where and as he does and adapting the novel both to the external conditions and the inner life of a member of one of those "primitive tribes," he shows us who may *really* have "the last word."

To take a more elaborate case, John Gay's *The Beggar's Opera* includes some sharp social commentary. After all, toward the end, the Beggar comments that, "Had the Play remain'd, as I at first intended, it would have carried a most excellent Moral. 'Twould have shown that the lower Sort of People have their Vices in a degree as well as the Rich: And that they are punish'd for them."[9] But Gay's work, for all its intentional reversals, finally remains so securely inside the formal and ideological guidelines of the canon as to be able to play with them. Brecht's *Three Penny Opera* extends these limits considerably in adapting Gay's story to social relations after the Industrial Revolution, and by considering those conditions from a perspective that is at once proletarian and experimental. These changes are part of the generational reformulation of a familiar story. To the extent that this story about class, sexuality, power, and reversed expectations claims that status, Brecht's representation re-presents a familiar *myth*. But Brecht is by now securely part of the European canon, too.

The noncanonical stage of the process occurs when Wole Soyinka transports Macheath and Polly to Nigeria in his *Opera Wonyosi*, combining them with traditional African and contemporary political elements to make a searing commentary on neo-colonial dictatorships. With "Mack the Knife" playing in the background, Dee-Jay, the narrator, opens the play with a rap on its title:

One time we called it the Way-Out Opera—for short, Opera Wayo. Call it the Beggar's Opera if you insist—that's what the whole nation is doing—begging for a slice of the action.

. . . You know what, why don't you just make up your own title as we go along because, I tell you brother, I'm yet to decide whether such a way-out opera should be named after the Beggars, the Army, the Bandits, the Police, the Cash-madams, the Students, the Trade-unionists, the Alhajis and Alhajas, the Aladura, the Academicas, the Holy Radicals, Holy Patria[r]chs and Unholy Heresiarchs—I mean man, in this way-out country everyone acts way out. Including the traffic. Maybe we should call it, the Trafficking Opera. Which just complicates things with trafficking in foreign exchange.[10]

As Dee-Jay segues into an Africanized and overtly political version of Brecht's lyrics, we are left to realize that the "opera" in fact has none of those proposed titles, but rather is named for "the famous Wonyosi," an absurd and absurdly expensive lace version of an African "agbada," which is to serve as the Emperor's (literal) new clothing.

As his play develops, it becomes apparent that Soyinka is simultaneously using and permanently altering the tradition, including the radical tradition, for he openly critiques Brecht's rigid class analysis in order to strengthen a position that is at once fiercely nationalist and what we in the Euro-American world would call liberal humanist. There is a sense in which Brecht, for all his formal iconoclasm and social radicalism, was a good son of his literary father, whereas Soyinka is a rebellious one, asserting a new and radically different reality.

Another example of what I mean might be the quest myth. Women of the metropolis and exotic peoples of both sexes often figure in quests, but as objects, not subjects. It is hard, in our cultural context, to imagine the female, rather than the male, serving as representative of the human spiritual norm, Everyone instead of Everyman, for the female, to us, remains Everywoman, and Everywoman is inevitably sexualized. Thus, in *Surfacing*, Margaret Atwood uses themes as old as the *Gilgamesh* epic, joining them with rituals from native Canadian Indian traditions, in an attempt to ally herself with *that* Outsider community, as well. Her quest as descent into the watery world becomes a metaphor for the fundamental female experience of childbirth—motherhood betrayed and finally accepted—creating a version of the thing that is new in an entirely different *dimension* of newness.

Dante recognized his debt to a long insiders' tradition when he created the special quest that is his *Commedia*. The role of Vergil both embodies and reflects the poet's sense of participation in a tradition. But Dante expands the tradition exemplified by Vergil's own use of the prophetic visit to the underworld by connecting human history and politics simultaneously to the largest spiritual forces in the universe and to the inner life of actual individuals. Those who have used Dante's themes have always built on this enlarged sense of the meaning of a journey to the world of the dead. In the twentieth century, the *Inferno* has spoken more directly to our inner life than either the *Purgatorio* or the *Paradiso*. When "outsider" writers make use of Dante's myth, therefore, it is not to take the tour of *any* part of the afterlife, but to show us Hell transplanted to the here and now, the social here and now, and its consequent distortion of individual psyches.

I think, for instance, of the way the American left-wing novelist Sol Yurick gives us a Brooklyn hospital as Inferno in his *Fertig*, in which the indifference, incompetence, and cruelty that kill the protagonist's child are played out and recalled in a setting that is consciously modeled on Dante's imagery, from the symbolic beasts on down to the frozen center.[11] More recently, Gloria Naylor's novel *Linden Hills* has been criticized for adapting the "white male Christian myth" of the *Inferno* to her allegory of black bourgeois life. Why not use African or Afro-American symbolic systems, one reviewer asked, instead of that same old high European culture? If there is a flaw in *Linden Hills*, I would not locate it in Naylor's extraordinarily powerful rendering of Dante's hellish vision. These characters are living in Hell, some of them at its very depths, and it is only fitting that the objective image representing their Hell be drawn from the demonic white culture in which they are all so heavily implicated and that constitutes their damnation as surely as Dante's characters experience their sin and their suffering as a single, organically organized concept.[12]

Clearly, there are many ways of appropriating the insiders' charter myths, the ones that were always *supposed* to be universal, as long as one accepts a particular definition of the universal human. For women, as I have indicated, even white, economically privileged Western women, certain of those myths are more readily adapted than others. But it is more problematic to consider whether women writing in the Western tradition may be said to have a characteristic myth of their own. If they have, I believe it is not rooted in the bodily difference between the sexes, but rather in the *social* experience of that bodily difference. More specifically, the myth resides in the cultural experience of being forcibly silenced and hence being left without access to language as a source of identity, a means of expression, or a modality of change.

Feminist writers and critics have adapted and retold the myth of Procne and Philomel as a representation of our condition. Jane Marcus's essay "Still Practice" is perhaps the most salient example of feminist critical theory built on this myth of women using the means available to them, speech denied, to tell of the brutal violation visited upon one of their number and on the sex as a whole.[13] Ovid tells us that Philomel, her tongue torn out by her rapist, makes a tapestry and sends it to her sister to show her what has happened. In *Titus Andronicus*, Shakespeare has Lavinia, who has had her hands chopped off as well as her tongue cut out, point with her stumps to the passage in the *Metamorphoses* that describes the rape of Philomel, using the text to explain her plight, and then, with her uncle's staff in her mouth, write the names of her own violators in the sand. To plunge from these sublime heights, another male author, John Irving, in *The World According to Garp*, gives us the actual experience of eleven-year-old Ellen James and the stupid, fanatical self-mutilation of the Ellen Jamesian feminists as complementary propositions in this same dialectic.

From Virginia Woolf's creation of Shakespeare's sister, equally gifted but born in a female body, to Tillie Olsen's discussion of motherhood and female creative incapacity in *Silences*, the emphasis on *not* writing, on being *prevented* from writing, underlies critical discussion of what is and has been written.[14] The next step in the theoretical process is for the female nontext to *become* the text, as in feminist treatments of Freud's *Dora*. As reflected in the lengthy bibliography to Bernheimer and Kahane's *In Dora's Case: Freud—Hysteria—Feminism*,[15] the obsession with this turn-of-the-century text, with its central *agon* between Freud and the hysterical adolescent girl who was his early patient, is not unlike the tradition's recurrent reference to classical myths. *Dora* may be our *Odys-*

sey and our *Metamorphoses* in one. The reason for this recurrence is that the principal symptom of the sexually molested girl Freud called Dora was aphonia. Freud tried hard to put words in her mouth—a proceeding that could be construed as benevolent only by someone entirely unfamiliar with our English idioms. From Hélène Cixous on out, however, feminist creative artists, critics, analysts, and historians have wanted to give the young girl back her own voice—and, in so doing, give one to all of us.

One of the things Alice Walker achieves in *The Color Purple* is to supply a voice to the inarticulate in a more concrete but also more sophisticated way. At the start of the novel, Celie is fourteen years old, barely literate, and with neither the vocabulary nor, seemingly, the capacity to describe her experience of rape by the man she believes to be her father. The rapist's words, which serve as epigraph to the first letter and hence to Celie's beginning to speak—"You better not tell nobody but God. It'd kill your mammy"—constitute the profoundly ironic permission to take the rape and (as in the Philomel myth, *Titus Andronicus*, and the feminist recreations of *Dora*) create a text out of one's own pain and oppression, written in one's own blood, if necessary.[16] The epistolary form, one of the earliest narrative strategies for the novel, is here appropriated as a source of empowerment for a woman who has no access even to the words that properly name violated parts of her own body. Some of us have always had our suspicions of Pamela—or rather of Samuel Richardson, even though he does get the sex and class dynamics right. Celie shows us why our suspicions were justified, as, taking hold of that pen to write first to God, later to her sister in Africa, and finally to "Everything," she becomes the black woman entering a world where telling is an *event* and writing can make something happen.

For, as the woman whose tongue is ripped out may find an unmutilated sister to tell her story, the woman writer at her best feels her hand guided, like Alice Walker's, by the woman who cannot write her own story because she cannot write at all. As long as, according to UNESCO, eighty percent of the world's illiterates are women, this is not a piece of pretentious rhetoric but a true responsibility. When the woman writer writes within the boundaries of what we already have been taught to recognize as literature, using, even participating in traditional canonical forms and myths, while asserting the specifically female myth, she surely extends our *common* literary heritage.

It is hard to disagree with Audre Lorde's much-cited dictum that the Master's tools will never dismantle the Master's house.[17] But people have to live in a house, not in a metaphor. Of *course* you use the Master's tools if those are the only ones you can lay your hands on. Perhaps what you can do with them is to take apart that old mansion, using some of its pieces to put up a far better one where there is room for all of us. One where no one asks me and I need not ask myself, as I talk about its fine proportions and human significance, whether I'm engaging in feminist criticism or the real thing.

NOTES

1. Ellen Carol DuBois, Gail Paradise Kelly, Elizabeth Lapovsky Kennedy, Carolyn W. Korsmeyer, and Lillian S. Robinson, *Feminist Scholarship: Kindling in the Groves of Academe* (Urbana, Ill., 1985). Ellen Messer-Davidow comments in a footnote (p. 102 n. 54 of the issue of *New Literary History* in which this essay first appeared) on the almost uniquely collective nature of this venture. The intellectual difficulties of collaboration were enhanced and complicated for us by the fact that, at no time after we decided to write a book "together," did all five of us live in the same place.

2. A version of this anecdote appears, with different applications, in my article "Feminist Criticism: How Do We Know When We've Won?"

3. The analogous and more destructive generalizations about *and from* the behavior of apes has begun to be roundly challenged by such feminist primatologists as Sarah Blaffer Hrdy. I do not know whether revisionist arguments are also being advanced in the case of the elephant seals.

4. *Cahiers de doléances des femmes en 1789 et autres textes* (Paris, 1981). The best source in English is *Women in Revolutionary Paris, 1789–1795*, ed. and tr. Darline Gay Levy, Harriet Branson Applewhite, and Mary Durham Johnson (Urbana, Ill., 1979). See also Paule-Marie Duhet, *Les femmes et la Révolution: 1789–1794*, Collection Archives (Paris, 1971). Duhet points out here and in her preface to the documents in the *Cahiers de doléances des femmes* collection that there are also a number of (readily distinguishable) "false" cahiers, petitions, and so on, purporting to have female authors, and she comments on the various motives—often satirical, conservative, antifeminist, or anticleri-

cal—behind this widespread assumption of the female persona. One distinction Duhet makes between real women and their impersonators is that: "Les femmes ont trop à dire . . . elles ne peuvent pas prendre la distance que suppose le maniement sarcastique de l'écriture. Leurs textes sont toujours marqués par une impatience, une indignation retenues, un souci de dominer les maux présents en y portant remède" ["Women have too much that needs saying . . . they can't achieve the distance presupposed by sarcastic handling of the written word. Their texts are marked by an impatience, a restrained indignation, a concern to surmount present evils by finding a remedy for them."] (p. 16, my translation).

5. See, e.g., in *Cahiers*: Anonymous, "Du sort actuel des femmes," pp. 115–23; Madame Grandval, "Pour les droits des enfants naturels," pp. 151–57; and "Doléances des blanchisseuses et lavandières de Marseille," pp. 43–46.

6. Jane Flax, "Postmodernism and Gender Relations in Feminist Theory," *Signs: Journal of Women in Culture and Society*, 12, No. 4 (Summer 1987), 629.

7. Chinweizu, *The West and the Rest of Us: White Predators, Black Slavers, and the African Elite* (New York, 1975).

8. Chinua Achebe, *Things Fall Apart* (New York, 1959), pp. 214, 215.

9. John Gay, *The Beggar's Opera*, 3.16.24–26, in *Dramatic Works*, ed. John Fuller (Oxford, 1983), 11, 64.

10. Wole Soyinka, *Opera Wonyosi* (Bloomington, 1981), p. 1 (scene 1).

11. Sol Yurick, *Fertig* (New York, 1966).

12. Gloria Naylor, *Linden Hills* (New York, 1985). Naylor herself offers a more dialectical view of the matter. When I mentioned the "white-male-Euro-Christian" critique to her in a public discussion at the University of Pennsylvania in March of 1986, she asked, as a former comparative literature graduate student at Yale, who those critics are to say Dante is *not* part of her "own" culture!

13. Jane Marcus, "Still Practice, A/Wrested Alphabet: Toward a Feminist Aesthetic," *Tulsa Studies in Women's Literature*, 3, No. 1/2 (Spring/Fall 1984), 79–97; rpt. in *Feminist Issues in Literary Scholarship*.

14. Virginia Woolf, *A Room of One's Own* (1929; rpt. New York, 1959); Tillie Olsen, *Silences* (New York, 1978).

15. *In Dora's Case: Freud—Hysteria—Feminism*, ed. Charles Bernheimer and Claire Kahane (New York and London, 1985), pp. 277–80.

16. Alice Walker, *The Color Purple* (New York, 1982), p. 11.

17. Audre Lorde, "The Master's Tools will Never Dismantle the Master's House," (1980) in *This Bridge Called My Back: Writings by Radical Women of Color*, ed. Cherríe Moraga and Gloria Anzaldúa (Watertown, Mass., 1981), pp. 98–101.

Between October 1988 and March 1996, I presented versions of this lecture at the University of Southern Maine; Barnard College; City College of New York; CUNY Graduate Center; Colgate University; University of Hawaii at Manoa; University of Hawaii at Hilo; Honolulu Community College; University of Kentucky; Hawaii Committee on the Humanities; University of Oregon; Southern Oregon State College; the Phi Beta Kappa Alpha of Hawaii Inauguration; University of Texas at Austin; Kyoto American Cultural Center; the Annual Meeting of the College English Association; University of Nebraska at Lincoln; Hastings College; University of Alabama; University of Arkansas; New York University; the conference on "Changing Directions in the Study of American Literature," in Pattaya, Thailand, where it was the keynote address; Virginia Tech; East Carolina University; the Wyoming Conference on English; Indiana University; and Goucher College. I have not included in the present version those sections of the lecture that *The Nation* excerpted and published as "What Culture Should Mean" (pp. 104–11). Once I'd written "Waving the Flag at Racism and Sexism" (pp. 127–38), I incorporated some passages from that lecture whenever I was asked to speak about the canon, but I have now put those back where they belong.

IN THE CANON'S MOUTH

In the academic year 1953–1954, when my brother was a college freshman, he commuted to a tuition-free branch of what is now the City University of New York, with his books and travel expenses supported by a State Regents Scholarship. Since he lived at home, he occasionally discussed aspects of his new studies with me. To an eighth grader, it all sounded very exciting, especially the humanities courses: art history, literature, writing. In his required first-year English class, one week, students were to select an essay topic from a list in the textbook. In my capacity as consultant, I helped him choose one, "I Live in the House My Grandfather Built." Now, my brother knew at seventeen and even I knew at twelve that this topic was meant to suggest a way of life quite different from the one we were experiencing ourselves, a way of life where one's ancestors had been Americans and property owners for generations in an environment of single-family homes that was distinctly non-urban, non-ethnic (definitely, non-Jewish), and non-poor, and that was based in a tradition of individual achievement and inheritance.

But, as it happens, we too lived in a house our grandfather had built—one of many, since he was a construction worker. Our grandfather—like yours, perhaps—loved to indulge in what my students in Hawaii called "talking story." Since he was the hero of most of his own stories, we had both heard repeated renditions of how, when this house came up for sale at a bank auction, Grandpa bid on it on behalf of our mother because, having worked on the construction site some twenty years earlier, he knew it was a well-built house at a good price. He would tell the story with as much pride as another man might show at having actually *bought* the house for his widowed daughter and her children. This pride of his and the repeated narration of the event reflected certain traditions that we were raised with, traditions of strong family feeling, hard-working union labor, collective work, careful bargaining for the one thing other than your labor power that you might ever expect to own, the house you lived in. They were traditions of immigrant working-class people. We knew that none of this was what would usually be inferred from the title "I Live in the House My Grand-father Built," but we thought it made an interesting and only par-tially ironic variation on the theme—an *acceptable* variation.

Well, the paper came back with no red circles signaling errors of grammar, usage, or spelling—we didn't *make* errors like that—but with a grade of C+—something also quite contrary to family traditions—and the single comment: "You have misunderstood the assignment; the topic was supposed to be about the influence of family tradition in your life." Okay, so this was bad teaching and most of us encounter some of that along the bumpy way to an edu-cation. But, bad teaching or not, it was, in fact, very effective in teaching us both a lesson, for my brother learned at seventeen and I at twelve that the family tradition from which *we* came was not the sort you were supposed to write about. Not in an English class. It didn't belong in the universe of letters, but rather was something you left behind when you entered college and thus crossed the bor-der into the Land of Culture. We didn't *come* from a culture, you see; we were only going *into* culture. Welcome or unwelcome, we were guests, fortunate guests.

It reminds me, nowadays, of the time in 1968, when I was a doctoral student at Columbia, that Lionel Trilling said that the Black students then occupying a university building should be granted amnesty for their breaches of institutional rules, although the whites should not. (He expressed no opinion, on the occasion, about the disposition of Hispanic, Asian, and Native American protesters.) The Blacks, Trilling told an emergency meeting of the faculty, were still "our guests, only halfway into the house of culture." Trilling has been dead since 1975, but I still want to ask him where he thought they'd been living before college if not in a house—a house, in fact, of culture.

Ten years before Trilling's remark, I went from the house my grandfather built—a house without many books, although it did have a kind of intravenous line to the public library—to the house of letters. As a product of the Advanced Placement English and Latin programs at a high school for intellectually gifted girls, I was well prepared for both the journey and the change of skins that it seemed inevitably to entail. Indeed, I greeted the literary education and the de-culturation it required with equal enthusiasm. Only more recently—since, say May '68—have I begun to rethink what literary education might be and whether it is possible to retain the sense of wonder without the mystification, whether culture might not belong to all of us, not in the form of a gift or an invitation, but somewhere we have (always already, and I can't think of a better place for this formula) participated in. I have not become tone deaf, but have rather learned to hear more voices—including, at last, my own. And I found—I increasingly find—myself baffled by the passionate tenacity of those other naturalized citizens of the Land of Culture whose patriotism remains unswerving and uncritical. It's their tenacity that interests me, here.

At William Bennett's early 1988 confirmation hearing for the Drug Czardom, one senator pointed out that the nominee had been "something of a loose cannon" in his previous posts. Now, Bennett's mission as N.E.H. Director, Secretary of Education, and co-founder of a right-wing educational foundation was always the promotion of a *tight* (not to say rigid) canon of the Great Books, so when I read that I giggled for a moment over the neat play on words. But the smile was wiped off my face a few weeks later when Dick Cheney, husband of the N.E.H. Director, was appointed Secretary of Defense. Since Lynne Cheney has been as ardent an exponent of the white male cultural tradition as her predecessor, this literal marriage of the humanities and the big guns made the cannon metaphor chillingly concrete.

Up to that point, those of us committed to curricular reform had found that pun both apposite and irresistible. I myself am the author of articles entitled "Their Canon, Our Arsenal" and "Canon Fathers and Myth Universe," as well as an appreciative reader of Robert Scholes's "Aiming a Canon at the Curriculum." There are several pieces, one of them a review of my own, whose titles play with the Tennysonian "Cannon to right of them, Cannon to left of them."[1] Henry Louis Gates, Jr. entitled his contribution to the debate *Loose Canons*, and *The Nation* for March 6, 1989, let us have it with both barrels: the article by Gerald Graff and William E. Cain is headed "Peace Plan for the Canon Wars," but summarized on the cover as being (or being about) "Canon Fodder." Later that year, the same magazine described a piece of my own ("What Culture Should Mean") as being about "canon culture." So it may be high time to make sure we know what this canon culture really is about and that we can tell the difference between a metaphor and a weapon, as those in power, both academic and governmental, continue to politicize an issue we'd always considered political in another, rather milder and more academic sense.

Those government officials, chaired professors, and Nobel Prize winners occupying the right battlement of the cultural bastion tend to speak as if the challengers have already won, as if I and others like me had hegemony. I confess this baffles me, for I'd always assumed that if I had hegemony, I'd notice. Back in my undergraduate days in the dorm, some of my friends, who had a good '50s book-knowledge of sex—which is to say, they knew the words, but not the music—would return from dates saying they weren't sure whether or not they'd had an orgasm. "Believe me," I'd tell them, "when you have one, you'll know it!" That's the way I thought it would be with hegemony: I'd know. But here were all these powerful people claiming the margins, where I thought *I* lived, because their rhetoric gained additional force from that position and the assumed outsider status justified their ferocious militancy.

But some of that militancy derives from the canon metaphor itself, independent of the gun pun. The literary application of the word makes ironic reference to biblical scholarship, where the books that constitute *the* Book are guaranteed as historically and philologically authentic; those that fail to meet the standards are not. ("Standard," by the way, is often given as a synonym for one meaning of "canon.") It is apparently not forbidden for the faithful to integrate material from the Apocrypha, the principal compendium of non-canonical books, into religious and cultural practices. Witness the annual celebration of Chanukah, based on the story in 1 and 2 *Maccabees*. Or the many representations in poetry, painting, and sculpture of Judith and Holofernes, Tobias and the angel, or Susannah and the Elders—all of them straight out of the Apocrypha. Apparently, stories from the Apocrypha are acceptable as narratives, but not as *texts*—not, that is, as sacred texts. In common discourse, however, as well as in established belief, that which is apocryphal, outside the canon, is *untrue*, inauthentic. An apocryphal story is a lie, possessing neither narrative nor textual authenticity. Whatever lies outside the canon defining authenticity must be *in*authentic.

When the biblical analogy was first applied to literary studies, it was in a very limited sense. The Shakespeare canon, for example, meant those plays that specialists generally agreed could safely and incontrovertibly be attributed to Shakespeare. (Or, with a nod to Prince, one might say, "The artist usually known as Shakespeare.") Although I use the adverb "incontrovertibly," there was, in fact, tremendous controversy over particular attributions. But it was *limited* controversy—as befits a limited definition. The self-conscious irony starts here, of course, for authenticating a play as the word of Shakespeare—even Shakespeare—is a far cry from authenticating it as the word of God!

So it doubles the irony when, working by what might be called analogous analogy, John Meyers's *The Seven Per Cent Solution*, a 1973 novel that purports to be a new Sherlock Holmes narrative by Dr. Watson, uses the word "canon" to refer to the set of texts by Arthur Conan Doyle that have hitherto been considered the complete Sherlock Holmes. (The Sherlockian canon, it's solemnly called.) The use of the term and the capitalization are both ironic—attributing to Sherlockians the same degree of scholarly weight and authority that characterize Shakespeareans, just as Shakespeareans and other literary specialists assumed the mantle of theologians in establishing *their* canons.

Back in the days when "canon" referred, by that biblical analogy, to the texts accepted as constituting a given author's body of work, we graduate students were nonetheless being introduced to the other body of works that is now called the canon. Then it was simply *the* (or "our") literary tradition. Although the tradition was old, we were taught, our collective sense of it did change over time. Individual books, authors, entire styles and schools might find less favor with "us" than with their contemporaries and vice versa. These changes were attributed to changes in taste or "sensibility," even though reference was also made to permanent aesthetic standards and qualities.

Those works that had best stood the test of time, which is to say, had been appreciated in a number of different periods with their different prevailing "sensibilities," were called "timeless," and appeal was therefore made to their universality. And the more things changed, the more they remained the same. That is, although the tradition changed in its components and its sense of their importance relative to one another, there was always *a* literary tradition, established and maintained according to generally admitted (and, inferentially, unchanging) standards of excellence—formal excellence.

Around 1970, when some of us began to look at this tradition from a feminist point of view, we noticed a general absence of a female perspective combined with a clearly gender-marked perspective, a male and masculinist perspective, in the work that was accepted as "our" tradition. Moreover, for many feminists, acknowledging the literary role of one social category, gender, raised questions about exclusion on the basis of race or of race and gender together. (Class tended to come later and differently.) We saw that the tradition was not only male but white and male and Euro-American in its makeup. I think it was at this point that the literary tradition started being called "the canon."[2] This usage had to do with a perception that there was a relationship close enough to be called an identity between who held social power and who dominated cultural expression.

We used the term "canon" as an educational tool, at first, to show up the way the traditionalists spoke sacerdotally, treating the Great Books of the Western World as if they were sacred texts and assuming the tone of a crusade in their approach to what was excluded. As the debate has escalated to a war, the traditionalist stand on the sacred texts has hardened into orthodoxy, what I think of as secular fundamentalism. So Saul Bellow demands an African Proust, an African Tolstoy—or nothing.

I recognize in this remark of his the full flower of something whose vestiges I still carry. For someone like me—from a non-religious, working-class, recent immigrant background—culture, high traditional culture, provided something to believe in and by which to redefine, re-create myself. It was a way to become part of what I saw as an elite above the elite of mere money or bloodlines. For a Jew, it was a way, perhaps, to become more WASP than the *goyim*. For a factory worker's daughter, it was the route to becoming free, classless, and urbane. I suspect I believed in culture the way my great-grandparents believed in the Messiah and with the same mediation of sacred text. And perhaps I tended to believe most of all in the modernist art of our own century, where form—in literature, textual form—is so often the dominant subject of itself.

I suspect, moreover, that I am not alone in this zealotry. Bellow, both Blooms—Allan and Harold—and a host of other Jewish males have suggested the particular way that I'm not alone, for high culture, to them, is clearly both a belief system and an object of veneration. As such, one of its features is that it entails membership in a community—not *in a* culture, but in the community *of the* cultured. The trouble with religious orthodoxy, though, is that, for everything it gives, there's something it takes away; for everyone it includes, there is a necessary exclusion. So I have felt it was important to free myself from orthodoxy, not by abandoning the love of literature (I can admit such an untheorized position because they can't evict me from postmodernism; it's my permanent address), but by accepting that the literature I love can come from many places, including the very places where people like me or like my students come from. In so doing, I believe I help bring together the culture defined by custom, ritual, daily life, material survival, belief systems—the anthropologist's culture—with the culture of books, plays, music, and painting—the critic's culture—in a way that frees and potentially empowers all of us.

Lawrence Thornton's extraordinary 1987 novel, *Imagining Argentina*, is a hymn to the power—the liberatory *political* power—of the imagination. Thornton's hero, Carlos Rueda, a dramatist and director of children's theater whose journalist wife has disappeared at the height of Argentina's military dictatorship, discovers that he has the uncanny ability to imagine the fate—the torture and present whereabouts—of the regime's victims. Telling the stories to desperate families is his form of resistance and would, in itself, constitute an impressive metaphor for the struggle.

But one day the wife of an internationally known professor, who had argued that "literature is always a kind of protest," comes to him to learn what has become of her husband. Carlos explains that, under torture, Professor Hirsch has indeed provided the information his captors sought, the names of fellow conspirators, but that this has proved a source of great confusion to the torturers:

> Oh, Hirsch gives them names, but they are never on the list. When they ask him about his friends he tells them that he is in league with Dostoevski, Koestler, Camus. That they meet in a place called The Castle. That they are members of a secret group, The Last of the Just. . . . What saved

Hirsch was his belief in the names even when the electricity was applied, the needle inserted, the cigarette ground out on his stomach, for he knew that the people behind the names had already experienced, or imagined, what was happening to him. . . . Hirsch believed in what the names said about what lay behind the pain, and that belief kept him alive.[3]

Earlier in the novel, the names and words of Wallace Stevens and Jorge Luis Borges, two writers far from "progressive" in the political sense, had been evoked to support the argument about the imagination. So when I got to the lines where Hirsch invoked Dostoevski, Koestler, and Camus by name, Kafka and Schwarz-Bart by allusion, I confess I stopped reading for a moment and addressed the author, who was a mile away from where I sat reading, "Larry, you mean the power of the imagination to liberate flows through these authors, too? That the canon can be a weapon?" And then I realized I had just made that pun, again, unintentionally and absurdly. But the question is not merely rhetorical, and maybe the answer should be, Yes, but it's not the only one and it must not be allowed to perform what *can be* its liberatory task by drowning out that other resonance, the voices of those who have hitherto been silenced or ignored.

NOTES

1. That review is reprinted in this volume (pp. 119–26). The issue of *Women's Review* in which it appeared ran two pieces on Paul Lauter's contributions to opening up the canon; the editors naturally called the one that preceded mine "Canons to Right of Us."

2. Paul Lauter's paper at the Retirement Symposium for Louis Kampf, held at MIT on March 9, 1996, attributes to Allen Grossman the first application of the word "canon" to the classics of Western literature.

3. Lawrence Thornton, *Imagining Argentina* (New York: Doubleday, 1987), pp. 159–60.

By mid-1989, I had already delivered the lecture "In the Canon's Mouth" at universities from Maine to Hawaii, and *The Nation*, in which I'd just published my first review, agreed to consider the lecture for publication. (I'd offered it, because I thought a leftist periodical needed something more partisan than Gerald Graff and William Cain's "Peace Plan for the Canon Wars," which embodied an early version of the notion of "teaching the conflicts.") Perhaps tired of the gun pun, *The Nation* retitled the excerpt published in its issue of September 25, 1989, taking the line from my remarks about Gloria Naylor's Shakespeare-in-the-park scene. I've never liked this new title, and it didn't improve matters any when a conservative panel at a recent conference was entitled "What Culture Should *Not* Mean." But the piece *has* been reprinted twice under *The Nation*'s title: once in the *Hawai'i Review* and once in a textbook (the 1993 edition of Oxford's *Popular Writing in America*), where it is paired for pedagogical purposes with a *National Review* article in which Sidney Hook bemoans "Civilization and Its Malcontents."

WHAT CULTURE SHOULD MEAN

Once upon a time the introduction of writings by women and people of color, both American and Third World, was called "politicizing the curriculum." Only *we* had politics, you see (and its nasty littermate, ideology), whereas *they* had standards. But nowadays, former Education Secretary William Bennett equates the modification of Stanford's Western Civilization (the required course) with the destruction of Western civilization (the social phenomenon); Lynne Cheney, chair of the National Endowment for the Humanities, sneers at universities that require students to take ethnic literature seriously; and the outgoing President devotes his last moments in office to excoriating the present approach to teaching history, with its trendy preference for critical thinking over mindless nationalism. Meanwhile, Christopher Clausen, head of the Pennsylvania State University English department, deplores the (dubious) fact that more undergraduates are required to read *The Color Purple* than the works of Shakespeare. And, I'm told, a winner of the Nobel Prize for Literature inquires rhetorically about the whereabouts of "the African Proust," apparently determined to bypass all African novelists until that one materializes.

Moreover—and notwithstanding elective and appointive offices, Nobel Prizes and university chairs—these assaults are couched in a discourse of marginality to some perceived radical hegemony. It is this claim to outsider, even guerrilla, status that underlies the aggressiveness of the attack. Now that those on the other side have so blatantly revealed that they have politics, dare we hope they'll recognize that we have standards? Apparently not, for we continue to be accused of adopting "sociological" criteria while they defend "universal values," the rhetorical weapons of choice being the compound verb "to throw out" and the pseudo-explanatory "simply because."

That is, those of us who want to expand (though I prefer to say enrich) the canon of great books and the curriculum based on it are accused of wanting *to throw out* the classics and replace them with works chosen *simply because* their authors are female, non-white or non-Western. The debate might be more effectively engaged if there were in fact a tendency in the reformist camp that proposed throwing out the entire received tradition. But as far as I know, the furthest we've gone is to propose adding to it and reading the whole tradition from a perspective informed by our sense of what is usually omitted and what that omission itself teaches.

"Throwing out" is, in any event, a rather abstract notion when it comes to the canon, which has no prescribed number of places within it. The curriculum, however, is indeed susceptible to "throwing out"; there, adding new material does entail squeezing or even eliminating other material. Well, *isn't* this "throwing out" the great books? I think not, because the real challenge is to their nature as required reading, and hence to the view that "every educated person" must be familiar with a certain set of texts in preference to other texts.

Accompanying the accusation of abandoning the great works is the charge that we are practicing a kind of literary affirmative action, a policy understood in this context to mean hiring or promoting the un- and underqualified. The application of the affirmative action concept and its concomitant "quotas" to this debate is apparently based on the assumption that no claim is being made for the new material as literature, and that certainly none could be sustained. We are said to be proposing the addition of new voices "simply because" of their gender, race or nationality, with no regard for the aesthetic values that had hitherto defined and (as it happens) closed the curriculum. A different aesthetic is presumed to be no aesthetic. And the female, black, working-class or homosexual experience is uncritically assumed to be, at best, an unlikely candidate for canonization, precisely because it is the marked variant, whereas the experience of straight white men has a unique claim to universality.

In fact, however, we have always maintained that the new material has literary resonance, acknowledging the power of literature to move, stimulate and transform human consciousness. So the actual difference between our respective positions is that we assume such literary power can come from a wide range of places in the culture and a wide set of social experiences, whereas they assume we are evoking values and power external to the workings of literature.

Meanwhile, can Saul Bellow really be waiting for the African Proust to materialize before he reads African fiction? If so, he's going to have to wait a lot longer and he'll be missing a great deal of wonderful writing. In the process, he denies to the African writer the very privilege he arrogates to himself of selecting a literary form and model appropriate to the enterprise. Despite all Moses Herzog's letters to the great male thinkers of Europe, Bellow's representation of the accumulation of the past in the individual consciousness is very different from that found in *A la recherche du temps perdu*. And surely (surely!) he knows that and believes it's acceptable. Or does he secretly think he's the Chicago Proust?

Even leaving Bellow's own fiction out of the equation, one might argue that Proust dealt with certain issues quite familiar to the contemporary African writer—the operation, for instance, of modernization upon an essentially tribal society. And it is as natural for an African writer to center a narrative on the installation or the aftermath of colonization as it was for Proust to focus on the Dreyfus affair. If it made sense for Proust as a Jew and a homosexual to dissect the invented Swann and the historical Dreyfus or the various inhabitants of Sodom and Gomorrah, it also makes sense for Chinua Achebe, Bessie Head, Ngugi wa Thiong'o, Mariama Bâ, Amos Tutuola, or Buchi Emecheta to tell us about the range of economic, cultural, and sexual confrontations between the native peoples and Europeans. As with opening up the American tradition, it is not because we owe it to the poor benighted Africans to give them some representation in an expanded definition of the literary tradition. Rather, we owe it to literature.

Well, maybe Bellow doesn't want to know from colonialism and neocolonialism and Third World debt peonage, even filtered through the inner life and sensibility of a single tormented individual. Arguably, he doesn't want to know about this stuff any more than the denizens of the Guermantes' drawing room or even the Verdurins' wanted to hear about Captain Dreyfus. But if Bellow grants French literature the right to have had a Zola as well as a Proust—and how can he fail in this retroactive courtesy?—it seems strange, to say the least, to deny an equivalent range to the emerging literatures of Africa. An equivalent range, but not an identical one. Africa doesn't necessarily need its Proust.

In the early 1960s, during the struggle over a national language for Tanzania, President Julius Nyerere translated *The Merchant of Venice* and *Julius Caesar* into Swahili. Critic Stephen Arnold maintains that Nyerere's translations assisted "the meteoric rise of literature in Swahili to its stature as a national literature today [while] . . . cautiously asserting that some things in the colonialist's culture might be of value in the formation of Tanzanian national culture." But most educated Westerners would smile rather than gasp at Arnold's notion of a "meteoric rise," and Bellow would remind us that there has certainly been no Tanzanian Shakespeare anyway, and that life is too short to bother with anything else, which is automatically understood as anything less.

Moreover, when a Third World writer does make use of symbols, myths and imagery from the dominant Western tradition, the variations are as important as the theme. It seems to me, for instance, that the Nigerian playwright Wole Soyinka may be seen as the African Brecht, although in the process of reinventing the filiation from John Gay to Brecht to himself, Soyinka proves a rather more refractory son of his literary father than Brecht was. A greater degree of deviation is required by his condition as a Western-educated black man in neocolonial Africa.

As someone with a grounding in the literary tradition, I confess I think the story about Nyerere translating Shakespeare into Swahili is rather charming. (Although I wish there were an audience for English translations of the Swahili literature his gesture inspired.) But I am also convinced that it is dangerous to proceed from there to fetishizing Shakespeare's purported universality at the expense of what might come from a black speaker of Swahili or English. There is no reason to assume that Shakespeare was any less grounded in his own history, with its particular opportunities and limits, than today's writers are. And we know that his history included not only the class, national, and cultural experience of Elizabethan England but also his membership in the male sex. For Virginia Woolf has told us what would have happened to that brilliant failed poet, his sister.

Some argue that Shakespeare is so universal we don't need the others, with their gender, race, and national blinders. The professor who complained about *The Color Purple* being taught in more required courses than Shakespeare thinks it's a shame because the Bard shows us a greater human range than Walker does. I am not prepared to concede even that, but if it were so, is there no value in being exposed to what Shakespeare leaves out of the range? Is there no point on the register of human experience where his approach is less than adequate? After all, his exploration of domestic violence, one of Walker's central themes, is *The Taming of the Shrew*. His victim of colonialism is the monster Caliban. His black man is the Prince of Morocco or Othello. His black woman, aside from a single nasty remark in *Love's Labour's Lost*, is nonexistent. Doesn't Alice Walker have something to tell us about "incestuous sheets" that *Hamlet* hasn't already covered?

The problem is, the universality argument is not usually made in terms of the range of human types and experiences the gentleman from Penn State invoked. The universality claimed for the classics is more often thought to reside in their general themes—where states of mind and spirit are understood as more universal than physical commonality—and the broad sympathy they express. This is the approach Lynne Cheney takes in her 1988 report *Humanities in America*. At one point, Cheney cites the passage in Maya Angelou's *I Know Why the Caged Bird Sings* in which the memoirist describes her childhood feelings about Shakespeare. She was eager to memorize one of his poems to recite at a church function, but she knew that her grandmother, with whom she was living in a small Arkansas town, would insist her piece be something by Langston Hughes or Countee Cullen, poets who spoke from the black experience. The words Angelou wished she could use to explain it to her formidable grandmother derive from this notion of universal sympathy. The adult writer, looking back, wishes she had been able to plead, "But I *know* that William Shakespeare was a black woman!"

I am not sure if this quotation from Angelou—the report's only reference to a noncanonical text—is a monumental misreading or an equally stunning example of bad faith. For the story as Angelou tells it actually begins with her rape at age 8 by her mother's lover. At the man's trial, she tells a lie to cover her sense of complicity in a previous incident of sexual molestation. As a result, the rapist is acquitted, and then murdered by the child's vengeful male relatives. Maya, packed off to stay with her grandmother in the South, learns the distorted lesson that her speech could bring about a death. So she remains silent for a year, talking only to her brother, until a sympathetic older woman lends her some poems of Shakespeare. The sonnet beginning "When in disgrace with fortune and men's eyes" speaks to the condition of the abused, aphonic 9-year-old. That's what she feels *she* is, in disgrace with fortune and men's eyes. The recognition of herself in those words makes her want to speak again and recite the words of this man who'd understood her. But she knows her grandmother will never understand wherein Shakespeare, too, was a black woman.

This story certainly has multiple meanings. It does not seem to me that one of them is that Shakespeare the great writer could read the heart of this black child, but rather that Maya Angelou, at nine and through all her pain, was an extraordinary *reader*. The incident hardly lends itself to the use to which it was put by the N.E.H. chair, which was to suggest that, although reading Shakespeare helped make the scarred child a speaker and eventually a poet herself, it is superfluous for us or our students to read Angelou—except to pick out specious morals about the timeless, placeless, personless value of the great books.

If we have to read black women's literature for moral lessons, I prefer the scene in Gloria Naylor's *The Women of Brewster Place* in which a community organizer takes a single mother and her too many children to the park to see an all-black production of *A Midsummer Night's Dream*. As they walk home after the enchanting event, one of the children asks, "Mama . . . Shakespeare's black?" And she replies, "Not yet." It's a nice idea, a black theater group performing Shakespeare for the children of Brewster Place, and it's also fitting that the militant organizer, who has adopted the African name Kiswana and whose boyfriend directs the troupe, is the one who encourages them to go. But Naylor is hardly telling us that exposing those kids to Shakespeare is the beginning or the end of what "culture" should mean to them. Shakespeare's not black *yet*. And when he is, it will not be because of the protean universality of a single white male born in Stratford-on-Avon 425 years ago, but because we all understand that although Shakespeare is dead, great poetry can still be written.

Most students will not turn out to be Shakespeare, whatever reading list their institutions enshrine. But the educational event we call empowerment is the same for both readers and writers. It is one that replaces a fetishized respect for culture as a stagnant secular religion with respect for culture as a living historical process, in which one's own experience is seen as an authentic part.

Most of the time, I do like the titles, puns and all, that *The Nation* gives to my pieces for them. That's the case with this one, in which Langston Hughes's line served as a joint rubric for two reviews that ran in its issue of July 2, 1990, perhaps in celebration of Independence Day. My review of *The Heath Anthology of American Literature* was paired with a review of a "bottom-up" American history. In reprinting it here, I've removed the Roman numeral they tacked on in the process. This piece actually had a substantive outcome: In 1992, Paul Lauter told my Summer Graduate Institute at the University of Tulsa that their instructor was responsible for getting Malcolm X into the next edition of *The Heath Anthology*. Apparently, no one had thought of it before!

I, TOO, AM AMERICA

A few years ago, I received a panicky telephone call from the humanities department at my hometown university: A computer error had left them without an instructor for Values in American Life. The course, part of the core curriculum, also satisfied the requirement (the *requirement!*) in American Ethnic and Racial Minorities. And, uh, the term started in a week. Could I possibly . . . ? Having just exhausted unemployment benefits from my last visiting professorship, I sure could. One small problem: The computer foul-up meant there were no textbooks on order. I'd have to compile a reading list that day and trust that rush deliveries would get me something to assign by the time we had finished with my photo-copies of Native American creation myths.

So yes, I wish *The Heath Anthology of American Literature* had been available back then.[1] In the absence of a collection that recognized gender, race, and ethnicity as literary categories, I faced a formidable book-ordering challenge. But it's the troubles that began once we *had* the books that give me some insight into the monumental achievement of Paul Lauter and his collaborators and that also raise some questions about their project's shortcomings.

That semester's streetwise students not only distrusted Thoreau, they maintained that they'd picked up their skepticism from me. (Some of my best friends are white male Harvard grads, and Thoreau, I was ready to swear, has always been one of my heroes!) They were crazy about Malcolm X. Even students who considered the humanities a conspiracy perpetrated by the institution, their instructor, and the authors on the syllabus read the entire *Autobiography* rather than just the assigned chapters. They came to class eager to argue about Malcolm's attitude toward women and how it might have evolved if he had not been assassinated.

As the term proceeded, the children of Chinese immigrants identified with the generational conflicts Anzia Yezierska depicts in *Bread Givers*, whose Jewish characters inhabit New York City's Lower East Side at the turn of the century. And it was a Chicana who was most moved by the story of Appalachian mountain people turned cotton-mill hands in Fielding Burke's *Call Home the Heart*.

Because conspiracy theories were never very far from my students' view of their education, they were often indignant about what had been omitted from previous reading lists and what they saw as having been forced down their throats instead. ("Why was it always Martin Luther King, Martin Luther King every year?" asked a redheaded woman with an Irish name. "Why didn't they ever teach us about Malcolm X?" To which a Chinese-American man responded, heavy with irony, "Why do you *think*?")

That all those voices are there *and we never even knew it* is the major revelation of *The Heath Anthology*. Not that the collection's bulk will suffice to answer those who resist challenges to the traditional literary curriculum by questioning whether there *is* any other material worth including. (Doesn't changing standards necessarily entail lowering them?) But the scale of the endeavor and the inclusion of so many black, Chicano, Native American and Asian-American authors of both sexes serve at least to demonstrate that, however effective the silencing of minority voices may have been, it was very far from total.

In itself, of course, quantity says nothing about excellence or universality or the combined tests of time and informed collective judgment. (Indeed, the other face of the disingenuous question about whether there is enough minority literature to afford a reasonable selection may well be that if the editors have found so much, most of it can't be any good—not "as literature," anyway.) Opponents of the enriched canon afforded by *The Heath Anthology* may try to attack it both coming and going, or at least through thick volume or thin.

The compilers had to cope simultaneously with the issues of quantity and quality, representative voices and aesthetic standards. But we readers can separate the strains to consider first, the breadth (and weight) of the contents, and then their depth, along with their several implications for how we understand the history and the milestones of American cultural expression.

The Heath Anthology does not ignore the authors, both major and minor, whom we expect to find in any survey of American literature. The 220 pages devoted to Hawthorne, for example, and the 184 to Melville include precisely the pieces by those writers that I was assigned in high school ("The Minister's Black Veil," part of *The Scarlet Letter*, "Bartleby the Scrivener") or in college ("My Kinsman, Major Molineux," *Billy Budd*), as well as less familiar selections that show something of each man's mind at work. But the rest of the section in which Hawthorne and Melville appear, titled "The Flowering of Narrative," is made up of works by Caroline Kirkland, Harriet Beecher Stowe, William Wells Brown, Alice Cary, Elizabeth Stoddard and Harriet E. Wilson, material that was ignored, deprecated, or unknown at the time I was required to take a year of American Lit. Similarly, "The Emergence of American Poetic Voices," which concludes Volume I, gives us almost equally thick chunks of Whitman and Dickinson, who are canonized in our contemporary sensibility, and also includes the schoolbook poets Bryant and Longfellow, along with more than twenty pages each of oral poems from Native American traditions and songs from both slave and nineteenth-century white communities.

The same mixture of acknowledged classics, popular genres and minority voices appears in virtually every section of the anthology. In fact, the only exceptions are those categories that, in themselves, represent a revolutionary rethinking of American cultural history—for instance, "Emerging Voices of a National Literature: African, Native American, Spanish, Mexican," encompassing eighteenth-century writers, or "Issues and Visions in Pre–Civil War America—Women's Voices."

It is here that the focus inevitably shifts from counting unfamiliar names to making aesthetic and pedagogical judgments. *The Heath Anthology* does not propose a countercanon from which names like Twain, Melville, Emerson, Hawthorne, and Faulkner have been expunged. But those authors have, inescapably, been given shorter shrift than they would be granted in collections that do not make room for such eighteenth-century women poets, black and white, as Bridget Richardson Fletcher, Lucy Terry, and Ann Eliza Bleecker, or their contemporaries of color, male and female, such as Jupiter Hammon, Samson Occom, and Francisco Palou. So real questions do arise about whether the new proportions are justified. Is the diet really enriched by the additions or have Lauter and his co-editors cut out essential nutrients only to replace them with junk food?

It is probably the proportions, in fact, rather than the inclusions, that will infuriate traditionalists. Particularly in the second volume, covering literature from 1865 to the present, most of the expected names are present but are attached to shorter selections than in the usual anthology; occasionally the pieces are arguably atypical of their work. Can an anthology really be said to be doing well by the recognized major writers when Fitzgerald is represented

only by "Babylon Revisited," Hemingway by "Hills Like White Ele-
phants," Faulkner by "Barn Burning" and "A Courtship"? What
does it tell us when, in place of more material by those important figures, we get their unexpected contemporaries: 130 pages of
poetry and prose from the Harlem Renaissance, as well as selections from Michael Gold, Albert Maltz, Clifford Odets, and Meridel
LeSueur?

If you are convinced that the only literary event of the 1920s and
1930s that needs to be taken into account was something called
Modernism, with the Depression relegated to the realm of mere
social history and the literature it engendered by definition minor,
then *The Heath Anthology* is a wasteful or even nefarious project.
If you think there is a straightforward and untroubled connection
between historical occurrences, popular movements, and literary
developments, then you will find much to admire in *The Heath Anthology*, but you may be made uneasy by strange-bedfellow formalist categories coexisting with the social ones. The rationale of the
collection and its constituent categories is never "either/or," always
"both/and." The abolitionist movement happened, the women's
movement was born, *and* prose narrative emerged; poetic voices
were tried out. There are connections, but they are not always obvious, and the contents of the collection do not reflect them in any
immediate or simple fashion.

The result provides a more complex sense than is available anywhere else of the way different meanings of the word "culture" are
related to one another and to texts. The anthology thus offers a
fuller and deeper picture of American cultures of the past. The
standard anthology fare is also transformed by this new context. Its
pre-eminence no longer unchallenged, it is open to a wider range
of comparisons and interpretations.

I say "American cultures of the past" advisedly, because it seems
to me that *The Heath Anthology* suggests a richer literary history but
a more partial and indistinct present. To epitomize one's own moment in coherent literary *and* social terms is a nearly impossible
task, and I suspect that many readers will take issue with the in-

clusions and exclusions in the book's final, post-1945 section. Among contemporary writers I regularly teach, for example, the following are absent from this collection: Angelou, Anzaldúa, Arnow, Bambara, Barrio, Kerouac, Malcolm X, Naylor, and Plath (as fiction writer). Meanwhile, my colleague who specializes in contemporary poetry complains that the choice of *which* recent white males to include with the women and poets of color is, at best, eccentric, with the sexagenarian Gary Snyder the *youngest* white male represented. (By contrast, the one who teaches American literature to 1865 exults, "It's not just that there are all those women and blacks and so on. They've got *Puritans* I've never heard of!")

A few cautionary notes for those who contemplate using the collection in the classroom: The headnotes, written by several hundred different scholars, are signed, which is rare and admirable, but students relying on them may not be able to distinguish between their presentations of biographical and historical facts and their subjective interpretations of texts. The explanatory footnotes obtrude, though they do not insult the intelligence or excessively distort the experience of reading. The only egregious errors are due to careless proofreading, resulting in irritating misprints and incorrect dates.

But most readers of *The Nation* are not in the market for an American literature anthology, progressive or reactionary. The reasons for anyone else to take an interest in this one are essentially civic. It should matter to all of us what versions of American culture are made available to those who will be consuming and also producing that culture in the chapter that could be called "New Voices: 1991 to the Present."

Envoi: As I write this evocation of the next generation, my 12-year-old son comes home from school. He is wearing bleached black jeans, a T-shirt, Italian sneakers that cost more than any pair of shoes I own, a Raiders cap and knitted black gloves without fingers. And sunglasses. I tell him I've been invited to address his middle school on the subject of poetry. "You're not gonna *do* it, are you?" Well, yes, I sort of thought—in fact, I'd start by talking about rap poetry. "I just don't think you know enough about today's culture," he concludes. I retreat to write this new ending. The sitter, a 40-year-old poet, knocks at my door. "I think you should know that your kid just asked if I liked video games when I was his age." How on earth do we learn *one another's* cultural history? *The Heath Anthology* is one essential step.

NOTES

1. *The Heath Anthology of American Literature*, ed. Paul Lauter (General Editor), Juan Bruce-Novoa, Jackson Bryer, Elaine Hedges, Amy Ling, Dan Littlefield, Wendy Martin, Charles Molesworth, Carla Mulford, Raymund Paredes, Hortense Spillers, Linda Wagner-Martin, Andrew O. Wiget, and Richard Yarborough (Boston: D. C. Heath, 1990).

Paul Lauter's *Canons and Contexts* is one of the most undeservedly neglected contributions to the culture wars. (When I think that *The Closing of the American Mind* was a bestseller . . . !) My review, which has some of the "I could just spit" quality of the preceding sentence, appeared in *Women's Review of Books*, Volume 9, Number 11 (September 1991).

. . . CANONS TO LEFT OF THEM

In the summer of 1964, I taught American literature in what is now called a "historically Black" college. At the time, we said "predominantly Negro." Either term covered the same reality: all the students were African American, all the writers we studied were lily-white. They were the usual canonical suspects, the male stars of the anthology that the students and I had jointly been assigned. American literature was divided chronologically, with the Civil War as its indispensable watershed. Since we were covering material up to 1865, any uneasiness I felt about the racial limitations of the subject could be waved away; after all, there wasn't any Black literature that early, was there? Certainly *I* had never studied any, and I held Ivy League degrees in English.

Service with the Southern Teaching Program was actually my second choice for how to spend that summer. I had wanted to join the Civil Rights movement volunteers in Mississippi working on voter registration and Freedom Schools. (I couldn't do it because I had to earn some money. My husband's academic-year fellowship was larger than mine, because he had a "dependent"—me—so to equalize the situation he would spend the summer writing his thesis, while I brought in enough to support us and make up the difference in our grants. We did this, I think, in the name of feminism.)

In Mississippi, that summer, the Freedom Schools based their "Citizenship Curriculum" on three questions: 1. What does the majority culture have that we want? 2. What does the majority culture have that we don't want? 3. What do we have that we want to keep?

Some students asked a fourth question: What do we have that we don't want to keep? Freedom School participants—teachers as well as students—were confronting in a positive way the same issues that presented themselves to me only as an absence, a lack.

It seems to me that the current struggle over the canon and the curriculum—the battle for what its proponents call multiculturalism, feminism, or enrichment, and its detractors label closed-mindedness, cultural illiteracy, or political correctness—started when those committed to the Civil Rights movement discovered that the version of American civilization our educational system transmitted particularly short-changed students of color, but offered students of all races a limited and distorted view of our common cultural heritage. I also believe that this discovery established the foundations on which the women's studies movement was built.

In *Canons and Contexts* (New York: Oxford University Press, 1991), Paul Lauter explores the canon controversy's roots in this history. (It's a history that is also his own, as a veteran first of the Freedom Schools and later of the Feminist Press.) The essays in this volume challenge the traditional canon from a feminist and multicultural perspective; they also discuss the politics of higher education—issues of budgets, cutbacks, and retrenchment, the misuse of part-time faculty, the betrayal of Affirmative Action—as the context in which the canon debate is being played out. In addition and almost incidentally, the book is a brilliant work of critical theory, one that eschews theoretical jargon in order to interrogate the discourses of texts and of criticism.

Canons and Contexts is divided into two parts. Their titles, "The Canon and the Literary Profession" and "The University and the Republic," lead one to assume—logically, but, I now think, erroneously—that the one is about canons, the other about their contexts. Even the epigraphs to the two sections bear out this assumption, for the first is "We'll build in sonnets pretty roomes," the second "I'd better consider my national resources." It is tempting to identify Ginsberg's resources as the base upon which Donne's pretty superstructure is built, but to do so is to miss some of the complexity of Lauter's intellectual method. For his point throughout is that cultural artifacts can never really be separated from their contexts, and that contexts are invariably contexts *for* cultural developments. So his discussions of the enriched canon never lose sight of the institutions and the society in which a new curriculum is being explored. And his analysis of the Bennett-Bloom-Hirsch axis of curricular traditionalists is part of his overall discussion of university management policies.

The aspect of the right-wing attack on the expanded canon that I find most infuriating is the know-nothing double whammy produced by the joint action of the phrases "to throw out" and "simply because." (You know the routine: we feminists and multicultural types want "to throw out" the entire received tradition, replacing it with literature chosen "simply because" it is the work of writers of color or of the female sex or both.) It took many of us a long time to realize that *they* didn't understand that we were claiming full citizenship for this new material in the polity of letters. We felt it should be read and taught because it had literary resonance; it did to and for us what literature does.

Lauter approaches the question of literary value by providing a series of extremely rich readings of noncanonical texts. "Every week," he tells us in the Preface, "I revive to hope and struggle reading and teaching Toni Morrison and Frances E. W. Harper, Rolando Hinojosa and Tillie Olsen, Charles W. Chesnutt and Louise Erdrich, Henry David Thoreau and Alice Walker." Hope and struggle cannot be nurtured, over the long run, by a list of the right names, nor is literature a compendium of pieties, slogans, and talismans. The real power is revealed only as you get into the texts, as do three of the central essays in *Canons and Contexts*: "The Literatures of America—A Comparative Discipline," "Reconstructing American Literature: Curricular Issues," and "Teaching Nineteenth-Century Women Writers."

By talking about its qualities as literature, Lauter simultaneously demonstrates that the newly introduced material is worthy of being the object of the full range of reading methods available for "high literature" and that reading it forces a challenge to those methods and the standards that they presuppose. He shows that the work of a noncanonical writer may, for instance, possess "complex poetic structures, ironic distance, or . . . the dense, allusive modernist line." But he also argues that "these are not the only virtues in poetry. Nor are they the only means for representing the modern world, much less 'our civilization'."

Far from throwing out the canonical works of white male authors, Lauter frequently pairs them, in teaching and in critical analysis, with works by women or writers of color. He reads in tandem Hawthorne's *The House of the Seven Gables* and Stowe's *The Minister's Wooing*, two quite different novels reflecting the legacy of Puritanism in nineteenth-century New England. Hawthorne's work, he maintains, is

> a sustained . . . an enclosed, meditation upon aestheticism outside history . . . Stowe's is . . . an effort to translate the values of a previous era into actions comprehensible to a contemporary audience. One might say that Hawthorne's aim is to create a "timeless" fable, a transcendent allegory, whose particular details are illustrative rather than defining. Stowe's book lives and breathes much more particularly in mid-nineteenth-century America.
>
> (p. 128)

But does being "timeless," in the sense of evading or transcending history, necessarily and appropriately translate into "timelessness" in the sense of classic immortality? In asking this question, Lauter clarifies some "alternative assumptions about literary value" that help us to classify and rank, and also simply to *read*, literature on both sides of the canonical-excellence line.

But *Canons and Contexts* is not—or not primarily—a book of literary criticism. Lauter invariably connects his observations about particular texts and types with the experience of bringing them into the classroom, so even the essays that focus on writers and their work are part of a study of American education that is as current as this morning's headlines. So when does education make the front pages these days? The two hot-news areas as I write this review are budget-slashing and curriculum change. In the past week, I've read about grassroots inner-city programs being cancelled for lack of money, state universities that still do not have their fall-term funding secured, and a controversial report recommending more emphasis on non-European contributions to American culture. Oh, and then there was the college president in yesterday's paper who worked for the CIA during his sabbatical and thinks that's entirely consonant with the mission of the university.

Paul Lauter's essays decipher the connections among events like these and juxtapose them with the arguments for reading the alternative canon. He refuses "to accept the notion that grudging, minimal change—stale slops from a military trough—is the best that American political leaders can offer," and insists that "a democratic [educational] polity and curriculum that values, indeed focuses upon, difference" will influence students so they cannot help wondering "whether the unique opening now before us will be foreclosed by dull, arrogant, visionless men of affairs, who have no language but that of war and no object but that of control."

The dull, arrogant, visionless men who manage military and governmental institutions run the universities, too. Lauter's essays from the early and mid-eighties about such issues as higher education's unimaginative response to (real or imposed) fiscal crises and its overly imaginative evasion of affirmative action principles are masterly in themselves. What makes his analysis unique, however, are, once again, the connections he draws, this time between budgetary and employment practices and curricular concerns. Bennett, Bloom, Hirsch, and their epigones are the intellectual allies of the arrogant, visionless men, endowing their efforts with all the pious sanction of an established church. By contrast, Lauter believes that "the primary goal of study, and particularly of literature, is to shatter . . . [the] 'woodenness' [of head and heart that Thoreau speaks of], to open our heads and hearts to what needs doing in a world near the beginning of its better history."

His essays on the cultural traditionalists lucidly point out how little their tracts have to do with a humanitarian humanities, and how much with the prevailing marketplace/managerial view of American society and the educational institutions that serve it. After all the verbiage that has been expended on the traditionalists, Lauter's "Looking a Gift Horse in the Mouth" (on William Bennett) and "The Book of Bloom and the Discourse of Difference" still add something new to the debate. But it is in his discussion of E. D. Hirsch, the quintessentially liberal exponent of cultural conservatism, that he is most pointed; "Whose Culture? Whose Literacy?" unmasks Hirsch's call for a common ground of communication, exposing its essential faith in the dominant culture for the bad faith it is.

To my mind, however, the two most important essays in the collection are those that, in the course of challenging the dominance of theory—or, rather, of a certain limited view of what theory is—lay the foundations for a radical new theory. When he cites the Freedom Schools curriculum, Lauter points out that it "asserted a fundamentally ethical understanding of education." He concludes "Canon Theory and Emergent Practice" with his own assertion that "For all the academic fascination with hermeneutics and epistemology, it is in the realms of ethics and politics that the question of the canon must now be construed." Rather than being categorically anti-theoretical, this essay, like the book as a whole, is a call for a more generous definition of theory. Lauter rejects the exclusive use of the term theory "to designate the various structural and post-structural forms of criticism currently being ground out by literary intellectuals [which] amount to an effort to appropriate to such writing alone what has become an academic honorific."

One problem with that appropriation is that it relegates the struggle over the canon to the realm of (mere) pedagogy or practice—even, on the part of those to whom only poststructural theory is radical, to the domain of the "liberal." Lauter reminds us, instead, that ethics and politics have their own theoretical dimensions, which do not have to be phrased in the jargon of discourse to count as theory.

In "The Two Criticisms—or, Structure, Lingo, and Power in the Discourse of Academic Humanists," Lauter (intentionally, I assume) evokes echoes of Disraeli on "the two nations" and C. P. Snow on "the two cultures" to argue, once more, that the dividing line between theory and practice, if there is one, is not where poststructuralism has established it. He begins the essay by mentioning three events that occurred within the overlapping worlds of theory and practice in the year 1966: the Johns Hopkins conference, "The Languages of Criticism and the Sciences of Man," that is generally recognized as the origin of poststructuralism in the United States; Stokely Carmichael's insistence that African Americans move from asking for freedom to demanding black power; and the offering of the first course on women within "the sanctified academic halls."[1] Lauter takes the conference on the one hand, and the black power-feminist impetus on the other, as representative of the two "movements" within contemporary literary study, movements that are both based in theory but in different theory.

These days, most popular books and articles about higher education read as if they're written by Lewis Carroll. Maybe Lewis Carroll with hemorrhoids. And my running commentary also tends to be rather sour, as the rhetorical questions flow like wine. "Hegemony? When did I get hegemony and how come I didn't notice it?" "Tenured radicals? I don't even have a fucking *job*!" "Politically *what*? Why is it suddenly worse to call someone a racist or a sexist than for him to *be* one?" *Canons and Contexts* returns us to the side of the looking-glass where things are by no means pretty, but where (to mix my crystalline metaphor) we see them face to face, illuminated, if not by mindless faith, by hope and love.

NOTES

1. Lauter cites Sara Evans's *Personal Politics* (New York: Vintage, 1980) as his source for the location of this course, which he says was held at the University of Chicago, with Naomi Weisstein as instructor. I am assured by a participant that it actually met at Loyola, where Weisstein was on the faculty, and am thus reminded that it is important to recall how little such institutions as Chicago (intentionally) contributed to the early development of feminist scholarship and teaching.

By March 1992, the culture wars had taken a particularly nasty turn, and it looked as if the right held all the cards. So I became interested in their ability to manipulate contradictory symbols so effectively. When I was invited to be part of a lecture series on censorship at Bates College—a series, I was later told, that had been established in expiation of some egregiously Incorrect act—I thought the time was ripe to examine how it came about that the right could censor with impunity while spreading around accusations of censorship with abandon. The lecture was enthusiastically received at the University of Southern Maine, the campus at which, three and a half years earlier, I'd premiered "In the Canon's Mouth." The following night, it bombed at Bates, where a rabbi in a red shirt argued that no one had successfully rebutted Dinesh D'Souza's wackiest claims (cf., for one, Alice Jardine, "Illiberal Reporting," *Women's Review of Books*, 9: 5 [February, 1992], 27–29), and that many Jewish women, like "their" men, opposed affirmative action. In 1993, I revised the lecture to take account of the fact that we were no longer living in the Bush League, but also to express skepticism, well justified, in the event, about the new administration. I presented this version at Wake Forest University and then put it away to await further developments.

WAVING THE FLAG AT RACISM AND SEXISM

The Semiotics and Politics of "Political Correctness"

A specter is haunting America. It is a specter with many faces and several names: multiculturalism, feminism, multiculturalism 'n' feminism, the closing of the American mind, political correctness. This ghastly wraith skulks through the end of this century and may continue to plague us into the next millennium. Indeed, Paul Weyrich of the far-right Committee for a Free Congress (a take-off on the old CIA-funded Congress for Cultural Freedom?) claims that "the politics that carry us into the 21st century will be based not in economics, but in culture." In my imagination, signs are going up all over think tanks like Weyrich's, adjuring the faithful to remember and act on the watchword "It's the culture, Stupid." Whenever this creepy fantasy visits me, I think back to the 1950s, an era when political correctness was enforced by loyalty oaths and blacklists, and when it would have been *a priori* evidence of my unfitness to lecture on a college campus that I began this talk with words that paraphrase the opening of the *Communist Manifesto*.

On the day in January 1992 that Martin Luther King's birthday was commemorated, I stayed home and watched a videotape of the entire PBS series *Eyes on the Prize*, a brilliant documentary history of the Civil Rights movement. An early episode showed the riots at the University of Alabama when a young woman named Autherine Lucy attempted to register there, while another showed boys and girls of just the age I was at the time walking through an angry mob of shouting whites and up the steps of Central High School in Little Rock, under the protection of federal troops. I thought about how I was scheduled to speak, some weeks later, about multiculturalism and political correctness at the Universities of Alabama and Arkansas. And I also remembered how, in 1960, when we picketed lunch counters at northern five-and-dimes in support of southern Black students who were sitting in, some sophisticates joked, "Oh, who'd want to eat at Woolworth's, anyway? The food's lousy and they can't even make a decent cup of coffee!"

But, back in the 1950s, no one was asking Autherine Lucy, who wanted to enroll in *library* school, of all things, at her home-state university, why she wanted to go to that lousy white institution or just what books she would make available to Black readers once she became a librarian. No one asked the nine Black teenagers in Little Rock why they were taking such risks to obtain the crummy white education available at Central High School. At the time, we believed it was not our job to teach Woolworth's how to make coffee, just to get equal access to it for everybody. And, although, in 1964, the Mississippi Freedom Schools did pioneer an approach to educating for social empowerment through cultural awareness and critique, we still didn't think it was our job to teach America's high schools and colleges how to make a curriculum that respects our various cultural pasts and is adequate to our future.

It's taken more than thirty years for those of us who work in educational institutions to understand fully that it *is* our job to teach these fast-food emporia of the mind how to brew us a nourishing and satisfying cup of cultural curriculum, one that, by recognizing race, gender, sexuality, and class as part of the cultural experience, would help all of us who come from houses without books—or without the books that hold sway on canonical syllabi and "cultural literacy" laundry lists—understand that we, too, come from a culture, a tradition that is a legitimate source of literature.

Watching *Eyes on the Prize* evoked the faces and events that were a part of every American's nightly news budget in the '50s and '60s, as well as a few that were part of my own history. I saw not only the anti-integration riots in Tuscaloosa and Little Rock, but the burning crosses, the firebombs, and the police dogs loosed on men, women, and children engaged in non-violent struggle for basic rights, and listened to the justifications of men in suits whose subordinates were in charge of the dogs and the firehoses, as they "explained" that the various Freedom Riders, school integrators, bus boycotters, and sitters-in were really the violent ones. It sounded familiar—surprisingly like the attack on political correctness made by those people who hold academic or governmental power.

Although *Eyes on the Prize* would always have been a moving experience for me, I found that viewing it on the very day in 1992 that the front pages of the nation's newspapers showed us George Bush linking crossed hands with Coretta Scott King and singing "We Shall Overcome" brought another image persistently to mind, the mug shot of "Willie" Horton.[1] Earlier that week, a colleague had cited Bush's attack on campus "political correctness," remarking that we—we who are trying to create a curriculum that recognizes and cherishes cultural diversity as a way to social change—might yet be the "Willie" Hortons of the '92 campaign. Well, it didn't happen, but here at the beginning of the Clinton administration, the cultural front is already heating up—for '96 and, as Paul Weyrich reminds us, for the next century.

Now, in the establishment and manipulation of symbols that substituted for argument in the 1988 campaign, "Willie" Horton—more precisely, the brooding and terrifying *face* of "Willie" Horton—was a very powerful sign, the embodiment of a racist nightmare that didn't even have to mask itself in coded euphemism, because he really *was* (or at least, he has been convicted of being) the rapist and murderer the myth says they all are, actually or potentially.

The other symbol that functioned in that campaign was the U.S. flag. (If you want to be macabre, you can call it Old Glory paired with Old Gory.) It was in the summer of 1988 that the Supreme Court ruled on the unconstitutionality of flag-burning laws, declaring that they criminalized a form of constitutionally protected expression. This gave the Republican campaign another handy icon, as Bush spoke out in favor of amending the Constitution to eliminate this particular protection of free speech and also took to visiting flag factories to demonstrate his devotion to the very productive process by which red, white, and blue cloth is transformed into the sacred object. For the discourse employed always involved "desecrating" the flag, and obviously only that which is holy to begin with is susceptible to desecration. To avoid the travesty of a constitutional amendment (or at least the political quandary of either having to vote for one or risk being labeled a heretic worthy of being burned oneself), the Democrats sponsored legislation making the same "desecration" a federal offense. A criminal offense.

At the moment of transition from the Reagan to the Bush administration, the outgoing president took the valedictory opportunity that his predecessor George Washington had used to warn the fledgling republic of entangling foreign alliances and that his predecessor Dwight D. Eisenhower had used to decry the "military-industrial complex" (thus introducing the term into our common lexicon or canon) to call for the teaching of American history in the schools as a way of inculcating nationalistic feeling, rather than the currently trendy critical thinking. (Note, please, that teaching mindless nationalism is not called politicizing the curriculum—teaching critical thinking is.)

With—or, at least, immediately following—this clarion call began the era of the chief executive whose campaign had pledged him to be the "Education President." Along with assaults on affirmative action and severe budget cuts, attacks on multiculturalism and feminism in the curriculum were the principal educational accomplishments of the Education President and his predecessor. Many of the attacks on curricular diversity came from government sources: not only from Reagan himself on that one memorable occasion, but from William Bennett as Director of the National Endowment for the Humanities and later as Secretary of Education, and from Lynne Cheney, his successor at N.E.H. The ideological underpinning for these policymakers' dicta came to a mass audience in a series of popular books like Allan Bloom's *The Closing of the American Mind*, E. D. Hirsch's *Cultural Literacy*, and Dinesh D'Souza's *Illiberal Education*; in speeches by such celebrities as the egregious Camille Paglia and others; and in articles in mass-circulation magazines from *The Texas Monthly, The Atlantic,* and *New York* to *Time* and *Newsweek*. I call the position they articulate cultural orthodoxy. It is the ideology that leads Paul Weyrich's assistant to assert that cultural conservatives must "seek to preserve traditional Western culture because it is *fundamentally true.*" (The italics are mine; the words, unfortunately, his.) The onslaught continues, whatever the educational and cultural policies of the Clinton administration, which has not, in fact, articulated an alternative position.

Meanwhile, in the spring of 1991, during one of his (relatively rare) appearances at an actual education institution, the University of Michigan, George Bush, the Education President, decried a sinister menace to free speech that had grown up on American campuses. The particular "political correctness" he identified on this occasion as the enemy of freedom was not the attempt to make the curriculum more culturally diverse. Rather, it was the rules that some institutions have established to control the use of hate language and other acts of symbolic violence against the members of groups identified by their race, religion, gender, or sexual orientation.

So the president for whom it was politically expedient (not to say, correct) to ban one form of free speech, attacks on the flag, expressed the ardent belief that it was wrong to suppress another form of free speech, bigoted verbal or symbolic attacks on persons. Now, the proposed consequences of damaging or destroying the flag are criminal penalties, fines and imprisonment, imposed by the courts after trial and conviction. By contrast, the penalties imposed by those colleges and universities that have attempted to regulate hate language are institutional, involving some sort of internal disciplinary process terminating, in the most extreme manifestations, in suspension or expulsion, but consisting at least as often of mandatory education in cultural or gender sensitivity. The direst fate, therefore, that can overtake someone found guilty of offensive speech is separation from the institution—the community's saying, in effect, that there is a minimal level of civility that all those who wish to remain members of it must adhere to.

I am not concerned—just yet—with whether establishing such rules is or is not a good thing. Rather, I am interested in the official attitude toward them of those who hold maximum power in the state apparatus. At best, it would seem that a president of the United States considered insulting the flag to deserve far greater punishment than insulting human beings. But the situation is not, in fact, "at best." It's far worse: The president of the United States was apparently convinced that it is *right* to make it illegal to degrade the flag and to impose criminal penalties for breaking that law, but positively *wrong* to impose rules against degrading other people with racist, sexist, anti-Semitic, or homophobic speech.

As a First Amendment absolutist, I always suspected the hate-language rules would do more harm than good. I believe there are more appropriate, non-coercive means available within an academic community to deal with expressions of hate, while continuing to make it clear how seriously the community takes them. But I also believe that this position has nothing whatsoever to do with academic freedom. At my own alma mater, Brown University, a student was expelled a few years ago for bawling insults against "niggers" in the middle of a residential quadrangle one night. When someone called out the window to remonstrate with him, he yelled at the "Jew faggot" to shut up. (You've clearly got your equal-opportunity bigot here.) Throwing this student out of college or, alternatively, applying a lesser penalty, ignoring the incident, or giving the guy a *medal*, would all be equally irrelevant to the freedom of intellectual inquiry within the institution.

What we are hearing, increasingly, in the attack on political correctness appears to be based on the assumption that it is far worse to call someone a racist or a sexist than it is for him to be one. It's based, also, on the dual assumption that the politically correct are quibbling only about words, which don't mean anything, and that the correct don't really care any more than anyone else (which is to say, themselves) about eliminating social evils. (Perhaps if the words "fighting racism" were substituted for "political correctness" in most of the diatribes against it, the opponents' real agenda would be apparent.)

Something akin to lip service is assumed to be at work in the use of ethnic, gender, and sexual identifiers in discussing works of art. Those of us who are currently being labeled "politically correct" have never made *arbitrary* choices among the aspects of non-canonical culture that we are interested in introducing into the curriculum. Our opponents assume that to say that a novel is the work of, for example, a young Chicana lesbian writer means to say it cannot be any good, cannot meet any recognized aesthetic standards. So they turn the rhetorical tables and argue as if those who are interested in commenting on, studying, and teaching the work of Sandra Cisneros, Gloria Anzaldúa, or Cherríe Moraga value them *only* because the authors are young(ish) Chicanas, two of them lesbians.

In fact, however, the aesthetics and politics of the situation are somewhat more complex: We do respect and value the experience and point of view of young Chicana lesbians and assume that their voices are worth listening to, that the *human* culture they represent is capable of producing culture in the expressive sense—art. But such respect means that we are open to recognizing art in that voice, not that any and everything in that voice is automatically and uncritically accepted as art. Those who use names such as Cisneros, Walker, and Morrison only as pejorative examples—as if the very citation of such names annihilates the multicultural position—are working from a rhetorical strategy that suggests that the name is enough to preclude the very possibility of cultural value.

It may be this reversal—the assumption that we use ethnic, gender, and sexual orientation descriptors for writers and artists as if they were *necessarily* honorifics because *they* use them as if they are pejoratives—that is responsible for another reversal that puzzles me. The defenders of monoculturalism (what you might call the one-crop cultural economy) resent references to the authors of the canonical Great Books as Dead White Euro-American Men. *Time*, for instance, excoriated a course on the American literary tradition for bearing the title "White Male American Writers"—as if only the marked variant, the female, the person of color, possesses a gender or a race that is worth noting or that has any connection to the kind of art produced.

Perhaps what they find threatening is the fallibility factor introduced into the discourse when acknowledged canonical figures are identified as having been shaped by their own time, nation, color, and sex. Once such fallibility is admitted, after all, the choice of these authors or artists could be seen *as* a choice, with other possibilities recognized and (who knows?) even selected. It may even be that the accusation of throwing out the classics so often leveled at the politically correct also has its origins in this business of descriptive identification. Just as, for them, identifying a writer as belonging to a non-white, non-male, non-straight social group is a call for continued and deserved obscurity, they may assume that we are invoking the same disappearing act for anyone we identify as a member of the dominant group.

The accusation of throwing out the landmarks of Western civilization is conceptually linked to the accusation of censorship that comes from the gag rules on hate language, for, once again, as with the flag rules versus the gag rules, it is the censors who are calling us censors. Actually, when it comes to aesthetic expression, it is very rarely the multicultural and feminist forces who are proponents of censorship. There are, of course, feminists who believe that pornography should be censored or otherwise controlled by law, just as there are other feminists who are very much opposed to such regulation. Many of us have also pointed out the obscenity of racism or sexism in artifacts of popular culture that are *not* pornographic, because the dominant commercial culture has tended to speak in the voice of those who hold power over the rest of us.

It is, in fact, precisely in the name of monocultural power that

actual censorship takes place. The "indecency" of Robert Mapplethorpe's photographic exhibit is patent only to those who are sure
they know what decency is for everybody. Probably more people
will *not* be sexually attracted by Mapplethorpe's sadomasochistic
images than are. But the question then is whether it's not art if it
doesn't turn you on. Or if it's not art if it does. The *New York Times*
for March 8, 1992, cites a letter to the editor of *Modern Maturity*,
the magazine of the American Association of Retired Persons. The
(presumably mature and modern) subscriber complained that *Modern Maturity* had sunk to publishing pornographic pictures, the
"porn" in question being an illustration to the article about the res-
toration of Masaccio's frescoes in Florence, specifically *The Expulsion of Adam and Eve from the Garden of Eden.* Almost anyone with a
traditional education in high culture would laugh at this judgment,
but some would nonetheless draw the line to exclude Mapplethorpe. There is not *supposed* to be any sexual content in the scene
of our naked (well, fig-leafed) First Parents being kicked out of
Paradise. If you see it there, it's a reference to the kind of sexuality
that is sanctioned by religious and secular conventions, the kind
that might stimulate someone who subscribes to those conventions.
So it's pornography according to at least one viewer because it refers
to (though it hardly can be said to *represent*) married heterosexual
monogamy. But Mapplethorpe's photos are pornography because
he both refers to and represents non-married, non-monogamous,
non-heterosexual relations, including acts of sadism. They get you,
so to speak, coming and going.

In a similar vein, denying funds to artists like the "NEA 4" who
are outspoken and iconoclastic in their approach to issues of religion, sexuality, and gender, precisely because they do challenge
dominant values, implies, once again, that those values are beyond
question, correct, and universal. Even if they are not so beyond
question and universal, the censors are going to do everything they
can to enforce them anyway, because the other values, those expressed by these artists, are clearly—well—*incorrect.* The role played
by the arts in the 1992 campaign, resulting in the removal of an
already conservative but apparently insufficiently reactionary Di-

rector of the National Endowment for the Arts and his replacement by an outspoken advocate of censorship, is part of this pattern. And, evoking memories of the political advertising and icons of the 1988 campaign, in 1992 there was Pat Buchanan campaigning against both the blasphemy and the obscenity subsidized by the Bush administration. (Oh: the problem was the censors weren't censoring *enough*.) The accusation of blasphemy again suggests an area where conformity to a monocultural ideal, that of Christian fundamentalism, is demanded. And where, at the same time, it is those who oppose that mind-control who are accused of wanting to do the "indoctrinating."

Now, just who is it that is refusing government funds to artists and scholars with whom they disagree about these sensitive issues and even proposing formal regulation of such artists? The politically correct? Of course not. It's none other than the National Endowment for the Arts, the National Endowment for the Humanities, and people like Senator Jesse Helms.[2] And if Helms is politically correct on the subject of racism and sexism, it can only be because "correct" has come to mean "right" in every sense of the word.

It has been a long time since avant-garde art and vanguard politics have had much in common. Twentieth-century American capitalist culture possesses a remarkable ability to cleanse all revolutionary art movements of *social* resistance while making a marketable commodity of formal rebellion. This pattern is most noticeable in the history of the visual arts, from the Impressionists forward, as what was meant to be revolutionary was adopted in the marketplace as fashionable. Two highlights from the career of the late Nelson Rockefeller, patron, collector, censor, and protector of modern art, are instructive from this point of view. One is the well-known clash between Rockefeller and Diego Rivera over the Rockefeller Center murals—where the rich boy's exercise of his power to censor was indirectly responsible for the destruction of a major work of modern art. The other is the far less well-known moment in which the best pieces in the collection of the Museum of Modern Art ended up spending the period of the 1962 Cuban

Missile Crisis in the Rockefeller family's underground vaults at their Pocantico Hills compound.

The fundamentalist right, which takes a dim view of experimentation in the arts and an even dimmer one of challenges to fixed religious, sexual, and racial ideologies, may be helping to mend the breach between art and politics. So, in its way, is postmodernism. Although, from one perspective, postmodernism is simply the latest avatar of the way art, theory, and fashion have worked together in this century to produce market-driven styles, it is also true that, by positing multiple sources and definitions of authority, postmodernism does challenge moral, political, and religious orthodoxies. Even though postmodernism is readily susceptible to being denatured of its political content, especially in the area of theory, where the *assertion* of radicalism often replaces radicalism, we can, once again, rely on the loonies of reaction to bring us all together in potentially productive (and even revolutionary) ways.

NOTES

1. In a *Nation* interview in which he protests his innocence, Horton points out that he has never been known as "Willie"—whence my quotation marks.

2. Preparing my text for publication in the spring of 1996, I come to a full stop at this line. As the Arts and Humanities Endowments are threatened with extinction, it is important to remember how recently they were the home of censorship rather than bastions of artistic and intellectual freedom.

Whereas the "debate" between Sidney Hook and me was arranged through placement in an anthology (see headnote for "What Culture Should Mean," p. 104), it was the editors of *Insight* who invited Carol Ianone and me to constitute a "symposium" on the literary canon. Because I was addressing a new audience, I repeated several arguments that also appear in "What Culture Should Mean" or "In the Canon's Mouth." Contrary to my efforts in the rest of this book, I have not deleted the repetitions here, since the rhetorical differences are of some interest. In *The Nation*, whose readers tend to agree with me on matters of principle, if not always on aesthetic questions, I feel at home. I relax and make jokes; I try for wit. At *Insight*, a publication of the (Moonie) *Washington Times*, I get serious and make points; I try for eloquence. Ianone, who achieved prominence through accusations that she was underqualified for the NEH oversight board, could be confident that, however weak her arguments, *Insight*'s readers were her people. It was not the kind of debate where we got to see each other's remarks before replying, but, under the circumstances, that hardly mattered; I could anticipate Ianone's points, and at least one *Insight* subscriber thought he could intuit mine without reading the piece. Thus, after the symposium appeared in the issue dated July 18, 1994, I received a letter from a subscriber, class of '47 at my own university. In the most breath-taking display of chutzpah I'd seen in a long time, he ended his diatribe by comparing himself to the "man on Calvary," praying, like Him, that I'd be forgiven, for I knew not what I did!

FIRING THE LITERARY CANONS

Last week, my son's English teacher denied Toni Morrison the Nobel Prize. Put less sensationally, what happened was that the advanced placement American literature class was told that Pearl Buck, whose work they were studying, was the only American woman to win the Nobel Prize for literature.

For those benefit-of-the-doubters who think she meant "the first," the teacher added that Saul Bellow was the last American so honored. I start with this incident because I believe it offers some common ground. For, wherever we may stand on the question of cultural traditions, none of us wants America's children to be taught—quite literally, in this case—that black is white.

The story also raises some controversial questions about why Morrison's work is not part of the standard curriculum and why a teacher's selective memory blanks out Morrison, whose *Playing in the Dark* challenges the traditional canon and how we read it, while enshrining Bellow, whose preface to Allan Bloom's *The Closing of the American Mind* defends the canon and insists that it alone is worth reading.

As a parent, I feel that my son and the other white teenagers in his class are being shortchanged, denied a part of our common cultural heritage, when their assignments include William Cullen Bryant but not James Weldon Johnson, Buck but not Morrison. (Yes, they also read the major white authors—Hawthorne, Emerson, Thoreau, Whitman, Melville, Dickinson, Twain, Hemingway, Steinbeck, Miller, Porter, Welty—but not Jacobs, Dunbar, Du Bois, Cullen, Hurston, Hughes, Wright, Baldwin, Hansberry, Walker—Alice *or* Margaret—Marshall, Gaines, Naylor. And no Kingston, Tan, Yamimoto, Anaya, Cisneros, Hinojosa, Anzaldúa, Silko, Momaday, Gunn Allen, either).

As a citizen, I am concerned that a just and decent society will remain an impossible goal as long as we continue to erase the range of voices from our culture. To do so implies that only those who already have social power have anything to say about human experience and its meanings, that only they possess the imagination, insight, and wit to say it well. On the global scale, I fear for a world whose cultural authorities argue that white Europeans such as Tolstoy and Proust are great writers, while black Africans like Soyinka, Bâ, Ngugi, Nwapa, Achebe, Emecheta, LaGuma, Tlali, Tutuola, Head, and Sembene cannot be worth reading because they are not Tolstoy but themselves.

But I am not just an outraged parent or a concerned citizen; I am a scholar and teacher who has been engaged for some 25 years in the effort to change and enrich the literary curriculum. This means I have taken the multicultural side in what members of my profession call "the culture war." We call it a war, and we talk about canons. We call one literary tradition a canon, and we make uneasy jokes about guns. For instance, there's my own title "Their Canon, Our Arsenal," Henry Louis Gates, Jr.'s *Loose Canons*, Robert Scholes's "Aiming a Canon at the Curriculum" and three pieces that play on Tennyson's "Cannon to right of them, Cannon to left of them." In the same martial spirit, columnist George Will compared the embattled role of Lynne Cheney, director of the National Endowment for the Humanities in the Reagan and Bush administrations, to that of her husband, who then was serving as secretary of defense.

Because both sides use military language with overtones of a crusade, I think it is important to understand what is invested in this war over the canon—starting with why it is called a canon. Only recently has the term had a literary connotation. Its original use in connection with texts was biblical: The canon is the set of books that make up the Book. This inclusion has a basis in scholarship, the application of certain standards—theological, philological, and historical standards—to a text.

But what of those that don't pass the tests? Many noncanonical religious stories are collected in the Apocrypha, which also has its place within Judeo-Christian tradition. The Jewish celebration of Hanukkah, based upon events narrated in the two books of Maccabees; the representation in Christian art of scenes from the books of Tobit or Judith; and poetic retellings of the story of Susanna all bear witness to the status of the Apocrypha in spiritual and imaginative life. Believers are encouraged to accept them as sacred narratives, even though they are not accepted as sacred texts. In our everyday spoken language, however, the Apocrypha doesn't come off so well. When we call a story "apocryphal," we mean it is not worthy of belief. It is inauthentic.

The term "canon" entered literary studies with a very restricted meaning—namely, all the works recognized by the appropriate authorities as being by some particular major author. So we had the "Shakespeare canon," the "Milton canon" and so on, with experts applying philological and historical standards to determine whether a given work could properly be attributed to the great man. This use of the word "canon" initially was meant as a mild, self-deprecatory academic joke, for certifying a play or poem as the authentic word of Shakespeare—even Shakespeare—is hardly the same as certifying it as the word of God.

This was the state of things some three decades ago. In those days, we also studied the body of literature that now is called "the canon," then known as the tradition, or our tradition. That definite article was very definite indeed: No other tradition need apply for consideration among the Great Books, for only this set bore the possessive adjective preempting questions about who "we" were.

The shift in terminology came when some of us began challenging those underlying assumptions, in the name of literature excluded from the list of "greats," particularly the work of women and people of color.

Now, I don't know which of my professional colleagues first referred to the classics as "the canon." But use of the term has expanded with the increasing challenges to tradition and consequent demonization of the challengers, assuring that it has had no chance to become a dead metaphor. The monoculturalists' approach to literary tradition as a secular religion also helps me to understand their attitude toward the included material (the sacred texts)—as when Paul Weyrich maintains that cultural conservatives should support the Western tradition because it is "fundamentally true"— and the excluded material (the nonsacred)—which must, like an apocryphal story, be inauthentic, spurious, and essentially *un*true.

A few years back, *Time* magazine quoted my observation that traditionalists treat culture as a "stagnant secular religion." A paragraph or so further, the article mentioned another professor, who called her course on canonical American literature "White Male Writers." In both cases, quotation replaced argumentation, since it was supposed to be self-evident that our statements were absurd. Making a case in this way is a symptom of secular fundamentalism in that it assumes a community of belief, with a shared conviction that certain views are within the pale and others ridiculously beyond it.

Multiculturalism makes the opposite assumption: that we have no single national identity or belief system but rather a set of diverse and sometimes conflicting identities and beliefs. Our cultural diversity is the result of a common history that we experienced differently. The painful divisions are caused by inequality and oppression, not by the cultural products that give form and voice to the pain and may help us understand one another. Everyone possesses a gender, a race, and a class identity, and saying so should not be regarded as sacrilege. Identifying an author as white and male is no more pejorative than identifying another as black and female. In neither case does the label sum up the author. Rather, it provides indications of the kind of cultural experience that shaped that person's consciousness and that the literary work may be expected to take seriously.

What is offensive is the assumption that only the nonwhite or nonmale should be so identified, should be the "marked variant." When the *Texas Monthly* attacked the English department at the University of Texas, faculty members were pilloried for advocating a multicultural curriculum in literature. Why, some professors would rather teach the works of Sandra Cisneros in an American literature course than an acknowledged classic such as *The Great Gatsby*, the magazine exclaimed. Cisneros was identified as a young Chicana writer, but F. Scott Fitzgerald, author of the "classic" text, apparently possessed no social characteristics—certainly none that shaped a novel that happens to be all about sex and class at a specific moment in American history. A classic is "pure," above race, gender, and class, above history.

The *Texas Monthly* felt free to dismiss Cisneros's books, *The House on Mango Street* and *Woman Hollering Creek*, which were never named in the article, as unworthy of a place in the canon or curriculum because their author is young, female, and Mexican American. In this and similar instances, no further argument is made than the pairing of certain tainted names, female and ethnic, with those of the inferentially sex- and race-free authors of "classics." (Cisneros against Fitzgerald in Gregory Curtis's *Texas Monthly* construction, Alice Walker vs. William Shakespeare in Christopher Clausen's *Chronicle of Higher Education* rhetoric.)

When the mere mention of a Cisneros or a Walker is expected to provoke hilarity or contempt, it is because those who laugh or sneer are convinced that great books cannot possibly come from such sources. The marked variant in an author's personal identity (female, black, Latina) reflects a marked variant in themes (marginal, particular, local), whereas the unmarked norm (white, male) writes about experiences that are general, human, and universal. And culture is about what brings us together, not what divides us, about commonality, not about difference. Or is it? The problem may reside in this definition, which is drawn from official culture, the civil equivalent of a state church. After all, when anthropologists speak of culture, they mean the texture and rhythm of life in a given society, all the ways human experience is organized. By contrast, monoculturalists promote a version of American culture that reflects only a piece of this larger definition, the piece accepted by those who hold economic and political power and who essentially are saying, "My identity is *our* identity."

In the official culture, the declaration that all men are created equal and possess certain inalienable rights looms large. Certainly, if you have to pay lip service to a civic ideal, I don't know a better one. But it is an ideal, and often it is only lip service. To behave as if this doctrine actually has been the guiding force of American life is to deny the historical realities of American experience, realities that have contributed to our actual culture, which is made up of a range of realities expressed in voices from all parts of that range.

Multiculturalism is not about these voices speaking only to themselves but about the complex interchange that makes up the whole. Mark Twain's *Adventures of Huckleberry Finn*, a mainstay of the American canon, is a novel about race relations, about slavery and freedom, written by a white man. As Shelley Fisher Fishkin points out in *Was Huck Black?*, Twain's sense of that story and his sense of the language in which to tell it were shaped by listening to African-American voices. *Huckleberry Finn*, in turn, freed up an American voice in both black and white novelists of succeeding generations. The cultural exchange goes both ways, and no single text encompasses it all. To treat *Huckleberry Finn* as if it were a sufficient summation—of either the race issue or the way to tell an American story—and to deny students access to the voices that Twain heard is to deny them access to an area of our common culture to which Twain's masterpiece is an opening. Fishkin argues that the "diminished voice" of Jim "must not be the only African-American voice from the 19th century that is heard in the classroom."

Calling *Huckleberry Finn*'s deployment of black voices "an act of appreciation, rather than appropriation," she adds that it *becomes* "appropriation to delegate to that novel the entire burden of . . . engaging students in questions about black-white relations in America. Our classrooms must be as open to an appreciation of African-American voices as was Twain's imagination."

In our own day, Toni Morrison's *Beloved* is a brilliant exploration of the meanings of slavery and freedom. Morrison's telling of the story is influenced by her reading of the Bible, of slave narratives—and of Twain. Her identity as a descendant of enslaved people is written into *Beloved*, and to ignore that cultural resonance is to miss some of what it is about. But to consider either the novel or its theme to be other than central to American culture, as *Huckleberry Finn* is central to that culture, is to distort our culture. And it is only a short step from that distortion to the next one, the claim that the king of Sweden didn't give Toni Morrison that medal in December.

In the headnote to "Treason Our Text," I mentioned two other pieces of mine that had been solicited and subsequently rejected. One of them was a contribution to the symposium on the influence of French theory on American feminist practice that was planned for the famous feminist issue of *Yale French Studies*. As a recent participant in the women's movement in France, I wrote about the possible influence of French feminist *practice* on American theory. The rejection letter proffered the curious explanation that the symposium had been canceled because of an excess of interest on the part of prospective contributors. Unlike Jane Gallop, who responded to her exclusion from this issue by psychoanalyzing its collective editorship to a fare-thee-well, I simply put my piece in the file and went about my business. (The business of being unemployed is a full-time job.) In 1981, when I translated two articles by Christine Fauré for the "French theory" section of *Signs*, I drew on some of the ideas I'd sketched out in that symposium piece and then, for a dozen years, as inept generalizations about "French" feminism gained increasing currency, I mourned the rest of my piece. (I could have been a contender, I kept thinking, I could have set everything straight!) So when Gay Wilentz invited me to contribute to the special issue of *Concerns* that she was co-editing, asking me to address the application of theory in feminist studies, I was more than ready. This article appeared in the Spring 1994 issue of *Concerns*, the journal of the Women's Caucus for the Modern Languages.

THE PRACTICE

An Immodest Proposal

OF THEORIES

What is the place of theory in Women's Studies? I won't guess at—which is to say, invent—the proportions, but there are many readers to whom this is a reasonable, even an anodyne question, and many others to whom it makes no sense whatsoever, particularly in a journal published by an organization allied with the Modern Language Association. For the latter, it will have a contradictory resonance; after all, isn't theory just another way of saying "feminism"? The counterpoised attitudes toward the subject I address here reflect a civil (well, a fairly civil) conflict within which feminist literary studies are held hostage: the division between those for whom "feminism" is primarily or even exclusively a way of reading and those for whom it is a way of apprehending and living one's (textual *and* extra-textual) life.

The critical approaches associated with these different definitions of feminism are usually—and, I believe, erroneously—tagged with the respective national labels "French" and "Anglo-American." The modalities called Anglo-American, Elaine Showalter's "gynocriticism," have links with—or at least openings to—feminist social theory. "Gynesis" (that is, the modalities often identified as French) posits literary theory based on postmodern linguistic and psychoanalytic models as the principal lens through which the entire universe of gender is perceived; this approach does not measure its relative distance from or closeness to social theory but rather positions itself as replacing or superseding it.[1] In the classroom, the two approaches confront complementary problems. The gynocritic can situate her work in the interdisciplinary framework of women's studies, but she operates from a disciplinary perspective at one remove from a theory based in historical and social relations. Her postmodernist literary colleague, by contrast, may teach and even create literary theory, but she is alienated from the feminist interdisciplinary context of Women's Studies as a whole.

To describe this situation is to take a stand on one side or the other, and my own bias has, I'm sure, been seeping abundantly through the seams of my prose. As a critic, I resist the intellectual synecdoche entailed in taking the part—that is, postmodern literary feminism—for the whole of feminist theory. When I say so in print I am often under the impression that I am actually doing theory, and I am astonished to learn that, in some influential circles, the very articulation of this position constitutes an "anti-theoretical" stance. Despite this bias and its at least disconcerting consequences, I believe that the division, especially when it becomes more of a gulf than a mere separation, has been premature. This essay attempts to get beyond the breach by suggesting some definitions and applications of theory that lie outside the boundaries of the debate as usually defined.

Taken as a whole, American feminist thought cannot *be* taken as a whole because, over and above the particular theoretical gap already mentioned, that thought reflects and then reflects *upon* the divisions of race, class, and sexuality that characterize our society. Gloria Anzaldúa's brilliant exposition of her vision of *mestizaje*, to take only one ground-breaking work by a U.S. woman of color— for we have a lot of ground to break—is at once a contribution to an autonomous theory of bicultural identity and to a polyvocal U.S. feminism.[2] But the generalization I was about to make when I was caught up short by my own phrase "taken as a whole" is that, although American feminist thought has engendered (so to speak) some new directions in theory, the greatest advances of Women's Studies as a classroom discipline have been self-reflexive; that is, they have been based on what is learned from the very practice of teaching Women's Studies in the academy, which means learning about pedagogy and, inseparable from it, theorizing about academic institutions and women's relation to them. So, as I attempt my end-run around the theory debate as elaborated in literary studies, I shall be carrying the ball (or at least the metaphor) through alternative theoretical taxonomies and also through the tendency of Women's Studies to institutional self-reflexivity.

In *Feminist Scholarship: Kindling in the Groves of Academe*, our collaborative analysis of the first decade of women's studies in the North American academy, my co-authors and I assert that our field possesses an "essential duality" owing to its being "rooted [both] in the disciplinary structures of contemporary intellectual inquiry and in a social movement."[3] Although our focus was on disciplines, we recognized that the institutional structure fostering and maintaining them was also in tension with feminism as an interdisciplinary modality and an activist movement. The theoretical dimensions of this tension are reflected in the way we structured our book's argument. The central section examines what feminist scholarship has to tell us about the origins and nature of gender oppression (in "Women's Oppression: Understanding the Dimensions") and the means to overcoming it (in "Liberation and Equality: Old Questions Reconsidered"). In this section we acknowledge that the category of "oppression" is fundamentally alien, if not indeed antagonistic, to customary academic discourse, and we go on to observe that remedies discussed under the radical rubric "liberation" tend to derive from scholarship that is not only interdisciplinary but also impossibly difficult to define in disciplinary terms, whereas work that supports liberal "sex equality" as a goal tends to be carried out within familiar disciplinary boundaries.[4]

Many feminist scholars have encountered situations in which inter- or extra-disciplinary knowledge created in the academy represents a threat that apparently has to be neutralized with reference either to its "really" belonging to some other discipline than the one with which it is chiefly identified—"sociology" is used as a slur in this way by specialists in literature—or to its defiance of all expected categories—"This isn't sociology or philosophy or political theory, so what is it?", the only possible answer being "Nothing." In short, unfamiliar knowledge, which tends to be more radical in its conclusions as well as in its categories, risks being dismissed as *not knowledge.*

For those of us trained in an academic discipline and committed, with whatever reservations experience has suggested, to the idea of a community of scholars, such resistance to new categories, connections, and findings comes as something of a surprise. But this negation is considerably less startling than the negation encountered *within* feminist studies on the part of those whose approach is informed by postmodern theory. *Feminist Scholarship* has been attacked by literary scholars for failing to consider theoretical as well as historical and empirical directions within Women's Studies. It is true that the book does not deal with literary feminist theory, partly because the developments it chronicles belong, as our introduction explains, to the 1970s, and partly because of my own identification, as the literary scholar among the joint authors, with the materialist theory laid out in the "Oppression" and "Liberation" chapters. It was undoubtedly an error of judgment for *Feminist Scholarship* not to address both tendencies within literary studies, since both were sufficiently developed by 1982, when we completed most of the research and writing for the book. I am now convinced that the book would be considerably more useful to colleagues in literature if it had included (which is to say, if I had advocated including) postmodernist "French" theoretical perspectives. But I remain astonished at the assertion by literary critics who work from such perspectives (some of whom reviewed the book) that its approach is "untheoretical." They take different theory to equal no theory, just as more traditional academics take inter- or extra-disciplinary knowledge to equal no knowledge.[5]

What is worse, it seems to me, is that concepts like "oppression" and "liberation" apparently have no place in literary feminist discourse. Since that is, by definition, a discourse of discourse, to have no place in it means to have no place, period. If these particular babies are allowed to go down the drain with the bath water, we have lost not just words but also feminist revolutionary knowledge, so that the discipline most concerned with words will have literally nothing to say in the global feminist project, in theory or in practice.[6]

One consequence of defining theory as coextensive with postmodernism and postmodernism as coextensive with French theory is that other *French* feminisms end up among lost actual and potential knowledges. More than a dozen years ago I referred to the work of Christine Fauré, a feminist of the post-'68 generation, as belonging "to a current in French feminist thought that has received little attention on this side of the Atlantic. . . . clearly to the Left of what many feminists in the United States have taken as the representative trend in French theory." I went on to insist on the importance of acknowledging

> that French feminist theory is more complex and considerably more contradictory than American journals have hitherto allowed us to see. . . . I believe it is essential to recognize that the conflicting theories do not exist in a social vacuum or even as the product of sectarian debate in a theoretically oriented movement. Rather, they coexist with—and either sustain or fail to support—an active and growing feminism whose manifestations assume concrete form as real French women struggle together to change their actual lives.[7]

The blinders that Americans have intentionally assumed with respect to French feminism are connected with academic Women's Studies and the knowledges it can generate. The roots of this relation lie in the differences between American and French feminist practice and the relation of each to the creation of theory.

The characteristic approach of American feminism is deliberately counter-institutional in that it not only counters existing social institutions but also establishes alternatives to them. The movement's formative years, the 1970s, were marked by a series of successive collective recognitions of one common social problem after another that society had proved inadequate either to name or to deal with, problems like rape, domestic violence, inadequate gynecological and obstetric care. The American feminist tendency was to say of each problem, in effect, "Okay, our society cannot meet women's needs in this regard. We will meet our own needs." This decisive turn away from the modalities of the dominant society—often, indeed, experienced as the modalities of dominance—was the origin of the rape crisis hotlines, battered women's shelters, and feminist health clinics operated on slender private resources and with largely volunteer labor that were and remain the most visible manifestations of feminist activity at the community level.

Establishing such alternative institutions, American feminism reflected its roots in a national (and also gendered) tradition of individual self-help and community participation, its rejection of the state as a potential, even an imaginable source of better lives for women, and its immediate connections to the alternative communitarianism of the New Left. These alternative institutions had obvious strengths, not only in meeting a perceived social need but also in carrying out their work according to the anti-authoritarian, non-hierarchical principles characteristic of the feminist movement. Their weaknesses are also obvious: inadequate funding leading to the burnout of under- or unpaid staff as well as a limited scope and a counter-cultural approach, both of which often kept the services from reaching the women whose need was most urgent. They demonstrated the difficulty of sustaining feminist modes of organization in a system that offers support only for their hierarchically structured opposite.

They do these things—to borrow a phrase from another context—so much better in France. Not, of course, in the France that has been presented to us as so unrelentingly theoretical as to be almost hypothetical, but rather in the France where actual women recognize the problems of their life and develop both practice and theory about how to confront them. *There*, the initial identification of a social need that has gone unmet by existing institutions may well lead, as it does here, to the establishment of an alternative institution. But part of the process of bringing such an institution into being is a demand that organs of society do what they have heretofore failed to do and provide public funds from the national or municipal government for its operation. Often the difficulty is doing so while avoiding the trap of becoming a political football between electoral parties eager to show their support for women and take over the new institution. In these circumstances, retaining feminist control and hence feminist human relations and organizational modes becomes the real challenge. Out of the experience comes not only a different sort of alternative institution with different relations to dominant institutions, but also a feminist movement with a different sense of women's relation to the state and, eventually, a different sense of the meaning of citizenship for women—I would go so far as to say a different *theory* of female citizenship.

The relevance of this French experience to Women's Studies is, first, institutional. In the United States, higher education has been the principal area in which perception of societal failure did not result in creation of a feminist alternative outside the dominant institutions. It did not because it could not. Community women's centers and similar organizations sometimes offer courses with academic content along with more practical ones, the knowledge of our own history and respect for our own writings having been denied to us as systematically (and systemically) as skills in auto mechanics or self-defense. But no alternative institution could have provided the research resources or the funding and certification that are essential to the enterprise of higher education. (A less lofty interpretation may be that those of us who were launched on academic careers as graduate students or beginning teachers were consumed with the desire to be professors in "real" institutions. But even were overweening ambition our only motive, there are few of us who haven't, at some especially tense or hateful moment, fantasized taking a position at Simone de Beauvoir College or Sojourner Truth University—if only they existed, if only they could exist.)

Whatever the motive or motives, the fact remains that those committed to working in higher education saw no alternative to doing so within existing university structures. Perhaps it is more accurate to say that we saw no alternative to doing so except *through* these structures. The problem, here as in France, has been to remain complicit with, even part of the dominant apparatus and yet continue to provide a critique of its organization and the content to which it gives rise.

One of the great strengths of Women's Studies, as the field has developed in American universities, is precisely in the area of institutional analysis, whether this has come through interdisciplinary study of such institutions as health, welfare, and media in their relation to women or through research and teaching within such disciplines as psychology and philosophy.

It seems to me that the astuteness with which French feminists have learned to deal with the state and its organs (male, of course) is potentially productive of a feminist theory of the nature of the state and the meanings of female citizenship. I believe that an American contribution to this theory can come from within Women's Studies, not only or even chiefly because Women's Studies is the theoretical arm of the feminist movement (a formulation that has always made me uneasy), but rather because of Women's Studies' peculiar (and peculiarly French, in the sense I have been suggesting here) institutional nature and its capacity to problematize and reflect upon that institutional identity as part of the theory that is, in turn, part of its intellectual content. The role of literary theory, understood in its largest (which is not necessarily its most imperial) sense, in such an undertaking is not as obvious as it is for the theory that reverses the relation of base and superstructure. This is by no means equivalent to saying that there is no such role but rather that it is at once more and less global than imagined. Just as Virginia Woolf had to learn, in *A Room of One's Own*, to speak in tongues like economics, tongues alien to her as a writer of fiction, in order to support her observations on women and fiction, so too might literary scholars in the academy try to figure out the relation of feminist criticism to the academy, to the particular institutional structures within it that enable us to engage in that criticism, and, beyond both, to the structures of linked institutions that constitute the hegemonic state apparatus.

Writing what is arguably the first and most powerful work of feminist critical theory, Woolf says a woman needs five hundred

pounds a year and a room of her own if she is to write fiction—
a process she wonderfully calls living "in the presence of reality"
(114). Due to the action of certain historical forces whose analysis
is part of our mission, some of us have come into possession of the
moral and material equivalent of five hundred a year and rooms—
even university offices—of our own. Some of us are even sitting
on chairs, an admittedly odd position from which to conduct a long
march through our institution or anywhere else. But if that phrase
is not to become synonymous with "working within the system,"
we must use these positions to work out a theory of our own practice and what it has to do with larger theories and larger practice—
with oppression and liberation, even.[8]

NOTES

1. These terms come from Elaine Showalter's elaboration of the difference.
My own position is that "in the long run, the principal difference [between
gynesis and gynocriticism] will be one of interpreting the nature of women's
marginalization from the power of discourse—whether that oppression origi-
nates in the symbolic system or in the social system that the symbolic system
reflects" (Lillian S. Robinson, "Feminist Criticism," *Encyclopedia of World Literature in the Twentieth Century,"* Volume 5: Supplement, ed. Steven R. Serafin and
Walter D. Glanze [New York: Continuum, 1993], p. 222).

2. Gloria Anzaldúa's work (see, for instance, *Borderlands/La Frontera* [San
Francisco: Spinsters-Aunt Lute, 1990]) does not stand alone, but is part of a
rich and growing body of theoretical writing by American women of color
like bell hooks and Patricia Williams.

3. Ellen Carol DuBois, Gail Paradise Kelly, Elizabeth Lapovsky Kennedy,
Carolyn W. Korsmeyer, and Lillian S. Robinson, *Feminist Scholarship: Kindling
in the Groves of Academe* (Urbana: University of Illinois Press, 1985), p. 2.

4. For the relation of "oppression" and "liberation" within and outside the
academy, see pp. 86–87 and 126–27. The term "extradisciplinary" does not
appear in *Feminist Scholarship,* though we do discuss a number of studies that
are hard to pigeonhole because they fall outside rather than across disciplinary
boundaries. An example is Batya Weinbaum's *Curious Courtship of Women's Liberation and Socialism,* which we cite on pp. 120–21 and elsewhere.

5. My co-author Elizabeth Lapovsky Kennedy extends this negative litany
still further in her article "In Pursuit of Connection: Reflections on Collaborative Work," *American Anthropologist,* 97 (1995). She points out that our experience over the years since the publication of *Feminist Scholarship* suggests
that the academy is so resistant to the idea of collective intellectual work that
the fact of our having all written the book together, which means that each

of us wrote the whole book, has resulted in no one's receiving credit for it. (It is the book *nobody* wrote.) I myself am frequently introduced by colleagues *with my c.v. in their hands* as an "editor" of the "collection" *Feminist Scholarship*. So a nontraditionally written feminist book becomes *not a book*. On the barriers to collaboration, especially across disciplines, see also my contribution to the Forum section of *PMLA*, 111 (March 1996).

6. In a review of two collections of feminist theory both notably lacking contributions by literary scholars, I point out that this erosion has already begun. See Lillian S. Robinson, Review of *The Politics of Diversity: Feminism, Marxism and Nationalism*, ed. Roberta Hamilton and Michèle Barrett, and *What Is Feminism? A Re-Examination*, ed. Juliet Mitchell and Ann Oakley, *Tulsa Studies in Women's Literature*, 7 (1988), 145–47. I am indebted to Teresa Ebert for the notion of revolutionary knowledges that contemporary "French" feminism has lost; see especially her 1994 MLA presentation and her book *Ludic Feminism and After* (Ann Arbor: University of Michigan Press, 1996).

7. Lillian S. Robinson, "Introduction" to Christine Fauré's "Absent from History" and "The Twilight of the Goddesses or the Intellectual Crisis of French Feminism," *Signs: Journal of Women in Culture and Society*, 7 (1981), pp. 68, 70.

8. In those volumes of the Bedford-St. Martin's series Case Studies in Contemporary Criticism that include an essay in feminist criticism, the general editor's introduction includes the statement "With the recovery of a body of women's texts, attention has returned to a question raised a decade ago by Lillian Robinson: Doesn't American feminist criticism need to formulate a theory of its own practice?" (For a recent appearance of this citation of someone apparently myself, see Ross C. Murfin's "What Is Feminist Criticism," in Shari Benstock's 1994 edition of Edith Wharton's *The House of Mirth*.) I believe I did not say and am sure I never meant to say any such thing a decade ago, but I say it now and am grateful to have the words put in my mouth.

Listening to Silences, the collection edited by Elaine Hedges and Shelley Fisher Fishkin and published by Oxford University Press in 1994, is an active tribute to Tillie Olsen and her critical master-piece *Silences*. It is "active" in that its editors and contributors are not content with paying respectful homage to Olsen's work, but proceed instead to invert, expand, and interpret in dozens of different directions the theory Olsen lays out. Although publication was delayed for some time, I honored the deadline I had been assigned and completed this essay about the range of political "speech" in late November 1991. "The Great Unexamined" still feels like a preliminary sketch of a larger theoretical project on which I have not yet embarked. I include it here because, even in this abbreviated form, it raises the question of class, the subject that is all too often the silent partner in the cultural discourse, even in discussions of silences.

"THE GREAT

Silence, Speech, and Class

UNEXAMINED"

Tillie Olsen's San Francisco apartment is directly across the street from the Chinese consulate. In June of 1989, during the student occupation of Tienanmen Square, this location gave her a literal window on the local response to events in Beijing. "The Chinese students were alone out there today," she reported to me, after we learned that the troops had fired, "but tomorrow there's a much bigger demonstration. Do you have a marker I can borrow to make a poster?" She came to my apartment a block away and I gave her my red marker. The next day, as we gathered in the narrow street in front of the consulate, hers was the only sign I could read.

For us non-Chinese, it was the most silent of vigils. We were surrounded by loudspeaker announcements—the latest news of the massacre—foreign chanting, and angry ideographs; but the only statement we could make was with our bodily presence. From time to time, my ear would catch a Chinese word I recognized: *we . . . shame . . . people*; it made a found poem. And every so often, over the heads of the weeping, shouting crowd, I would glimpse Tillie's sign. DENG XIAO-PING, it cried out, red on white, DO NOT DE-STROY CHINA'S BEAUTIFUL FUTURE. Inspired, I went back to my apartment for the other marker, the black one, and made a poster of my own. Where Tillie's was lyrical, in her style, mine was ironic, in mine: A PEOPLE'S ARMY DOESN'T SHOOT DOWN THE PEOPLE. And I returned to the demonstration. A group of Chinese students read my sign, bowed, and silently clapped their hands as they passed.

Like any good postmodern narrative, this anecdote authorizes speculation in a number of different and sometimes mutually contradictory directions. I am particularly interested in (not to say preoccupied or obsessed with) those that suggest the political dimensions of silence and speech in the overlapping universes of discourse and action. I have sometimes used it, an anecdote about two posters—actual *signs* at a moment when theory allows us to describe anything as a "sign"—to illustrate a lecture about the literary canon and multiculturalism. Perhaps, I mused, it is precisely this sort of literary influence, the "chain reaction of the empowered subject," that traditionalists are afraid of.[1] But, postmodern or no, I had to mutilate the story to make it fit my rhetorical rubric. That particular chain reaction matters because neither Tillie Olsen's writing nor mine is restricted to hand-made placards. Yet our writing does acquire some of its meaning from the interruptions, the necessary silences entailed in our activism. We are the kind of activists we are because we are writers, but we are also the kind of writers we are because we are activists.

More important, just as contemporary literary theory has enabled us to conceive discourse as action, it should make it possible for us to understand action as discourse and thereby to read political action as a form of articulation, rather than its absence, as speech rather than as silence. In other words, if this essay had an epigraph, it might be a testy, belligerent, "You lookin' at me? You lookin' at me? Who you callin' The Inarticulate, anyway?"

The word *circumstances* recurs throughout *Silences*. It is Tillie Olsen's way of characterizing the conditions that hamper creative life without resorting to value-laden jargon. "Circumstances" is a—well—*circumstantial* description, one that makes ready connections between external facts and the internal history they shape. It also conveys a certain flexibility. Not only do circumstances alter cases, but circumstances themselves alter and, with them, the meanings attached to social experience. If we are not equally free to create our own expressive destinies, neither are we necessarily the silent victims of history.

"Circumstances" is also—and I think usefully—imprecise, covering the joint and several actions of gender, class, and race with family, work, and political structures. There is no vagueness, however, about the hard material facts and their impact on the making, unmaking, and nonmaking of writers. In the years since Olsen first began speaking and writing on these issues, both feminist and multicultural studies have emerged as complex and powerful critical forces. They have developed in tandem with the changing creative situation of women and people of color and have simultaneously helped to chart the change and participated in the cultural process. *Silences* itself has become part of the rich and raucous history of breaking silence about the cultural realities of gender and race.

But what about class? Olsen's term *circumstances*, despite its apparent neutrality, was one of the critical tools that familiarized American readers with the cultural conjunction of sex, race, and class. *Silences* is usually characterized as a study of or meditation on women and writing, hence about gender. Olsen's observations on the situation of black writers—especially the quantitative exercise in which she examines how few blacks, as of the mid-1960s, had managed to publish a second book after they'd brought out one—also strike the imagination and remain in the memory.[2] The sensitive reader of *Silences* will also be able to recall passages about the physical and spiritual weariness that impede the creative development of working people. In the brief passage called "Creativity: Potentiality. First Generation," in the section entitled "Deepenings, Roundings, Expansions," Olsen also considers the internal barriers that keep the working-class writer from coming to the written word.[3] And Olsen's own affinities as writer and critic are clearly proletarian as well as feminist.

Still, what *about* class? In contrast to race and gender, class is a critical and analytical category without a coherent voice of its own. Working-class experience not only silences those who live it, but silences the culture about class itself. Class is thus the Cinderella of cultural studies, left behind in the ashes (the literal dustbin of history?) while race and sex whirl off to the ball.[4] It is what Olsen herself, in the phrase I have borrowed for my title, calls "the great unexamined," thereby recognizing an interpretive silence about the phenomenon of mass silence, as if all we needed was this shame-faced metasilence.[5]

In *Silences*, Olsen describes the time- and spirit-consuming labor of housework and child-rearing, especially combined in the "double day" with jobs outside the home, and charts the toll exacted by working-class jobs in general, a toll very much at odds with the enabling conditions for the production of literature. But she tends, in so doing, to take an evolutionary view of the relation of class to literary production, one in which the children and grandchildren of the proletariat have access to some of the educational and creative opportunities that make it possible for them to write from within a working-class experience and community. It is this process that provides Olsen with her term "the first generation," which she frequently uses, in *Silences* and elsewhere, to describe the background of particular writers and also to identify promising literary trends or movements in the making. Thus, *Silences* is dedicated both to "our silenced people, century after century their beings consumed in the hard, everyday essential work of maintaining human life. . . . Their art . . . refused respect, recog-

nition; lost" as well as to those of their descendants "by our achievement bearing witness to what was . . . silenced." It seems to me that
it is time, as part of that process, to acknowledge and honor the
widest possible range of expression as the speech—the articulate
speech—of the oppressed.

In a provocative paper at the 1990 MLA convention, Michael
Bennett hypothesizes a "poetics of divestment."[6] The divestment he
refers to is not another negative state, a silencing, like disinheri-
tance, disempowerment, or inarticulateness. Rather, he is using the
term in the specific and localized meaning it acquired through the
political activism of the 1980s: the movement to get foreign institutions to "deaccession" their shares in companies that do business
in South Africa. Because American universities hold stock portfo-
lios, much of the divestment activism in this country centered on
campuses, with students and faculty applying pressure to the institutions' corporate decision makers to end their economic complicity in the policies of apartheid. Bennett's paper draws a parallel
between the development of the divestment movement as he experienced it at the University of Virginia and the evolution of African-
American critical theory. On both sides of the parallel, the issues
of empowering an authentic voice of the oppressed and learning
to hear it effectively were foregrounded.

But the divestment movement was manifested in a series of actions that may themselves be characterized as symbolic speech, and
Bennett's discussion hints at, although it does not elaborate, a cultural theory that would understand the ways that form and content
work together in such actions. In the Virginia scenario, I was particularly struck by Bennett's description of the concentric circles of
protest and protection created by the supporters of divestment. After listening to presentations at a student-sponsored divestment forum, the finance committee of the university's governing board

> refused to engage in a dialogue or make any commitments toward a policy
> review. This refusal triggered a sit-in which was amplified by the presence
> of several hundred protestors outside who had been attending a simulta-
> neous public rally. . . . These protestors formed a human chain around the

Rotunda, significantly slowing the process of the eventual arrest of those inside.

Ironically, the arrest of the "Rotunda 31" was also slowed by the presence of a group of suit-and-tied academics who were occupying the room until 5:00 to hear a distinguished historian deliver a paper touching on First Amendment rights. So the conference-goers sat in chairs placed around the students sitting on the floor and proceeded with their business.[7]

When he summarizes the history that culminated in this multifaceted demonstration, Bennett notes as one important stage the construction of a campus shantytown during a 1985 board meeting. He refers to this initial shantytown, which the broad coalition of divestment forces was to rebuild at every subsequent board meeting for the next five years, as "our first foray into *symbolic language*." And, when he mentions the lawsuits over the movement's right to build shanties next to the Rotunda, a certified historic landmark, he calls the shanties "an effort to bring the *voice* of black South Africans to Charlottesville."[8] Thus, for Bennett, the "symbolic language" of the shanties expresses the "voice" of black South Africa. Although his analysis does not pause to acknowledge the metaphorical character of this "voice," I believe that it is precisely here that the poetics of political action has its most profound application.

The construction, occupation, and meaning of the shanties that went up on many American campuses in the 1980s were themselves a form of political speech—speech, moreover, that was representative, rather than directly communicative. When black South African workers put up shantytowns, it is for the purpose of utilitarian shelter in the urban areas to which they are restricted. The shacks are not a symbol of deprivation for them, they are part of the actual deprivation, miserable housing. When privileged American students place replicas of these shanties in the shadow of ivied walls and ivory towers, the shanties, whatever their scale and suitability as residential accommodations, are translated into symbolic statements. Even on campuses that cannot boast landscaping and architecture as splendid as Virginia's, there was always an eloquent contrast between First World institutions and Third World living conditions. But it is the immediate economic connection between those institutions and the conditions elsewhere that support and enable them that makes the eloquence effective. This is the case even in the bitterly ironic situations where the elite campus is located in the middle of an urban ghetto or where local homeless people use the shanties for shelter against the elements. (In fact, the difference between a shantytown in South Africa and one at Penn, Columbia, or Chicago is like the difference between homelessness and street theater.) And the contrast persists on campuses where Olsen's "first generation" is being educated and where it is a narrower version of academic privilege that is nonetheless supported by the labor of black South Africans.

This is not to say that South African blacks, any more than other oppressed people, lack the capacity and the means for symbolic speech. But, just as university students and faculty with all the resources of verbal rhetoric at their command still opt at times to create an architectural representation of oppression (or to occupy the administration building as the local *locus* of power), oppressed people select a medium appropriate to their condition, one that may or may not rely in the first instance on verbal discourse. It seems to me that the failure to recognize this full range of representation as political speech seriously falsifies the meaning of social and cultural resistance. The falsification has its own full range of dangerous consequences from, for instance, the tendency to equate dissidence with the activities of writers and intellectuals; to the imposition of narrow definitions of what constitutes a "prisoner of conscience"; to the assumption that the American blacklist victims of the 1950s were primarily or exclusively writers, directors, and performers in the entertainment industry. The literal danger inherent in each of these consequences should be obvious: by privileging one form of resistance over another, all of them tend to expose some of the most oppressed among us to further attack. Less directly, they can also have the effect of replicating the hierarchy of class within movements designed to resist it. Ultimately, they displace logocentrism from the universe of abstract theoretical polysyllables to that of potentially lethal weapons against those whose principal language is not necessarily language.

So far, however, in my own effort to avoid privileging the literary text over other forms of political speech, I have made a number of unwarranted assumptions. All working-class political texts may deserve to be read with the full range of interpretive attention, but it does not necessarily follow that all literary texts emanating from working-class experience can be read through the same political lens, particularly if that lens is one of self-conscious militancy. Tillie Olsen cautions the writer of the first generation against adopting the themes and tonalities of the dominant literature. But she does not reject the idea of "literariness" itself, which entails a vision of political speech that is often complex, covert, and subtle in its execution.

As a literature of the first generation—a "literary" literature, that is—emerges into being, not only can its politics not be read as if they were a poster painted in primary colors or written in "big character" ideographs, they often subsist at some remove from the discourse and even the possibility of activism. Far from being one means of political activism, contemporary American working-class writing often presents itself as a substitute for an activism that has been superseded, frustrated, or defeated.

Two recent anthologies, *Calling Home* and *Overtime*, embody different—and differently gendered—aspects of this phenomenon of surrogacy.[9] Janet Zandy's collection, *Calling Home*, brings together writings by American women of working-class origin from the whole of the twentieth century. It includes a generation of women who write (or are represented in the volume by oral histories or other forms of nonwritten witness) from the direct experience of the proletarian job, neighborhood, family, and culture, and a generation of women who are from working-class backgrounds, but whose development as writers coincides with if it does not directly reflect some distancing from that background. The difference, as I understand it, is between those of an earlier period for whom everything is problematic *except* their identity as women of the working class, and their descendants, for whom working-class identity is itself the (great, unexamined) problem. The very title, *Calling Home*, suggests that the subject, wherever she may be, is located somewhere other than at home and is attempting, through the act of making literature, to get back in touch with the place she is from. The tone is one of loss and the pain of remembering what has been lost, underlying a sense of not fully belonging anywhere. If long-distance telephoning means reaching out and touching someone, the someone most of Zandy's contributors are trying to reach is themselves. Zandy's introduction reflects her own awareness that the process she calls "circling back," even if possible and complete, is not sufficient, that the justice to be done to working people is material and historical, not only, or even primarily, textual. But she leaves unstated the possible connections between the narrative of working-class women's experience and the advent of that justice. The experience of estrangement at the center of so many of these narratives strongly suggests that, far from being a stage in the process of militancy, this writing could come into being only in the absence of collective struggle.

American resistance culture is informed by the politics of race, where the assertion of identity constitutes a challenge in itself, and the exploration of identity is a form of community action. The evocative power of *Calling Home* also resides in the search for identity, but raises troubling questions about whether, in the context of *class* identity, that search is the beginning of resistance or an acknowledgment of its end.

Overtime makes somewhat the same point, in a more overtly masculine register. Although its subtitle, "Punchin' Out with the *Mill Hunk Herald*," implies a certain level of activity, if not of activism, that activity is chiefly one of valediction. *The Mill Hunk Herald*, published by Pittsburgh activists throughout most of the 1980s, served as an outlet for worker-writers around the country, chiefly male blue-collar workers from the "rust belt" cities of the industrial North. As a periodical, it was not only an outlet for personal narrative, but also a focus for action based on that narrative, specifically the rearguard action of fighting the plant-closings, sellouts, and give-backs that characterized the death agony of heavy industry in the United States. Selected from the periodical and collected into a book that won the Before Columbus Foundation's American Book Award, the pieces become something else: a statement of culmination.

In the mid-1980s, local director Tony Buba, with the cooperation of the *Mill Hunk* staff, made a film with and about the unemployed and soon to be unemployed steelworkers of Braddock, Pennsylvania. The footage ends with a pitch for the *Mill Hunk*, shot on the tracks leading to the defunct steel mill. Gesturing at his Lech Walesa Solidarity T-shirt and mentioning the mutual support of the two movements, the editor says, "See this guy? He's crazy enough to organize in Poland. We're crazy enough to organize here in Pittsburgh!"[10] The big difference, of course, is that Solidarity won state power, while the American industrial workers lost even their oppressive base of action.

From the point of view of reading the discourse of working-class political action on the international level, Solidarity might have been a better case in point than the South African liberation struggle. I chose the latter because its discourse included a wider range of symbolic support activities on the part of Americans and others outside the country or the immediate frame of reference: symbolic activities that were nonetheless able, as with the shantytowns, to link the conditions in South Africa to a refusal on the part of First World activists, particularly within academic institutions, to benefit from those conditions. Americans also lent support to Solidarity but, except in the case of the *Mill Hunk* collective, they tended not to perceive and dramatize connections between their own situation and that of the Polish workers. (Indeed, few of the Americans who waxed enthusiastic about Solidarity experienced or identified such links as the commonality of alienated wage labor under state and "free market" forms of capitalism. And, of course, some of the most ardent wavers of the Polish flag were also ardently anti-labor, not to say anti-worker and anti-resistance, in their own country.)

The words and actions of Solidarity count as literature only in the expanded definition of political speech I attempted to outline earlier, whereas the contributors to *The Mill Hunk Herald* and its anthology were consciously making literature out of the stuff of their lives. It is tempting—if depressing—to relate this difference to the other difference, the one between success and failure. In a recent interview, the editor of the *Herald* and of *Overtime* confided that his then wife had criticized his continued attachment to the project, which she saw as a lost cause within a lost way of life.[11] "What do you want?" she would ask. "To be the one who stays behind at the steel mills to turn out the light?" My own reply to this rhetorical question would be, "Why not? Somebody has to." Ultimately, *Overtime* is not only the chronicle of the decline of heavy industry in the industrial heartland, but the successful translation of that death into cultural expression.

So the female voices that are calling home in Zandy's volume are the voices of regret for the past. The male voices in Evans's collection (overheard while punching their time clocks at the close of work, not *hitting* out at those responsible) are the voices of farewell. Jointly, both groups are the heirs to generations of ancestral silence, of attributed inarticulateness, and they find their own voice only in an essentially negative declaration. Despite their removal from the working-class experience, however, or *its* removal from them, the new first generation of writers of both sexes has not become something *other* than working class. Rather, they are moving, along with our entire social structure, into a new series of class relations that does not yet have a name, but where the same conditions of alienation and exploitation, the same denial of human creative potential, continue to prevail. In this sense, their empowerment through the word and the empowerment with which their writing endows their readers do not come too late, after all. It comes at the beginning. And it comes *as* the beginning.

NOTES

1. I included this anecdote in some versions of the lectures entitled "In the Canon's Mouth" (pp. 94–103) and "Waving the Flag at Racism and Sexism" (pp. 127–38).

2. Tillie Olsen, *Silences* (New York: Seymour Lawrence-Delacorte, 1978), p. 9.

3. *Silences*, pp. 261–64.

4. This line comes from a discussion of Spike Lee's 1991 film *Jungle Fever* in "Straight Out of Hollywood," my lecture on that film and on Ridley Scott's *Thelma and Louise*.

5. *Silences*, p. 264.

6. Michael Bennett, "The Poetics of Divestment/The Politics of Voice," presented at the Annual Meeting of the Modern Language Association, Chicago, December, 1990.

7. "The Poetics of Divestment," pp. 1–2. Michael Bennett generously gave me a photocopy of his typescript at the close of this conference session without knowing who I was or what use I planned to make of his work. Rather than repay this generosity by siccing a bunch of *sics* on a text meant for oral delivery, not for publication, I have taken the liberty of correcting obvious typos.

8. "The Poetics of Divestment," p. 9, emphasis added.

9. *Calling Home: Working-Class Women's Writing*, ed. Janet Zandy. New Brunswick, NJ: Rutgers UP, 1990. *Overtime: Punchin' Out with the Mill Hunk Herald*, ed. Larry Evans. Minneapolis: West End Press, 1990. See also my review of Zandy's collection and of the Cornell ILR Press's reprint of Teresa Malkiel's 1910 *Diary of a Shirtwaist Striker* in Lillian S. Robinson, "Class Acts," *The Nation*, 251, 14 (November 12, 1990), 570–72.

10. Tony Buba, *Lightning Over Braddock*, 1988. When I interviewed Larry Evans, he showed me videotaped clips of several scenes, including this one, from Buba's film. I understand the scene does not appear in the final edited version.

11. Lillian S. Robinson, interview with Larry Evans, Baton Rouge, La., July 21, 1991.

My two lectures on the canon eventually became a mass of intertextual spaghetti, so frequently was I borrowing passages from each to fill out my arguments in the other. So I thought that, once I disentangled them, I would have a version of "Waving the Flag at Racism and Sexism" that I could bring up to date for this collection. But once I separated the strands, I saw that "Waving the Flag" stands on its own as an artifact and a record of its moment, and that what was needed was not an update, but a parallel essay from the perspective of the Clinton years. Portions of the resulting piece were presented as part of my contribution to the symposium on "Teaching Politics and Literature," held in March 1996 to honor Louis Kampf on his retirement from MIT.

THE CULTURE, STUPID

January 1993. Like his hero, John F. Kennedy, Bill Clinton invites a poet to take part in the inauguration. For once, at least, the bankrupt label of "role model" has some meaning, since Clinton apparently did learn from JFK just which muses are fittingly invoked as an American president assumes the office. Kennedy, of course, selected Robert Frost for the job, whereas Clinton chose Maya Angelou, each of the poets being associated with the incoming president's native region. Kennedy—also "of course"—picked a poet whose canonical status was already beyond question and who was already old enough to be ossified as a "beloved" national institution among those who associated poetry chiefly with required English classes, which they didn't usually love at all.

By contrast, Angelou, although a more accomplished performer than Frost (no sun in the eyes would stop *her*) is a controversial figure. With her slender poetic reputation, her autobiographical writings so widely read and taught but also so often censored, her professorial chair under intermittent attack, Angelou literally embodies the interrogation of cultural certainties that has marked the decades between the two inaugurations. As an African American and a woman, she could be read as a walking avatar of multiculturalism, even if her poem were not, in itself, such a forthright celebration of diversity. As it is, her words, as well as her presence, bespeak a politics that embraces differences and posits a richer social fabric based on that embrace.

I didn't watch the inauguration from my hotel room in Bangkok, but, the next day, I included Angelou's inaugural poem, "On the Pulse of Morning," in the reading I gave at Srinakarinwirot University. It was certainly the latest in multicultural experiences. My copy came from the *International Herald-Tribune*. When I returned to the States, I learned you could dial up Angelou's own rendition on my local newspaper's voice-mail information line. And people were doing it. They were actually calling up to hear a poem.

A few weeks later, I heard Angelou speak to a capacity crowd, many of them doubtless drawn to the event by her recent publicity. She addressed the students directly, invoking the range of ways their ancestors had arrived on this continent. Whether in chains through the Middle Passage or to escape oppression in the form of pogroms, famine, or dictatorship, she told us, they had paid our dues at the university, loving us in advance. Her version of multicultural education was to adjure the students to live up to that love and, more programatically, not to leave college without having read some Black authors. And some Shakespeare. And some French literature. It all belongs to all of us.

Angelou's speech was an ideal lead-in to my own more modestly presented and attended lecture the next evening, a version of the pieces published here as "In the Canon's Mouth" (pp. 94–103) and "What Culture Should Mean" (pp. 104–11). This lecture was part of my campus interview for an endowed chair, and the head of the search committee said in his introduction that they'd been attracted to my candidacy because of my commitment to challenging the canon. Despite these encouraging signs, when I set out, around that time, to update my 1992 lecture "Waving the Flag at Racism and Sexism" (also included in this collection, on pp. 127–38), I was certain that the issues I'd identified in the last months of the Bush administration were not going to evaporate in the more hopeful climate of the new regime. I was smart enough to know the culture wars would continue, but not sufficiently clairvoyant to anticipate the form the battles would take over the past three years. Perhaps I should have augured more from the fact that I didn't *get* that job. I still have a sneaking fondness for the inaugural poem, though.

In the spring of 1993, when I imagined and inserted into "Waving the Flag" that right-wing think tank whose walls, echoing Clinton's campaign line on the economy, were admonishing the fundamentalist faithful that "it's the culture, Stupid," I suspected that the next campaign had already begun. Although there was ample evidence to support my fantasy of the sign, I think I saw it more as a cartoon in *The Chronicle of Higher Education* than a reality we'd soon be confronting. But it was, in fact, from a berth at the American Enterprise Institute that Lynne Cheney, former Director of the National Endowment for the Humanities, spoke out against the proposed National History Standards and called for abolition of the Endowment itself. Surely, it would have taken more than a caricaturist's vision to foresee former Education Secretary William Bennett, Cheney's predecessor, churning out best-sellers by packaging tales from the more pious classics in age-targeted volumes, each canonical item with its moral neatly attached.

When I called my earlier essay "Waving the Flag at Racism and Sexism," I meant to speak literally, as well as metaphorically, about the manipulation of imagery and the way it effected the sacralization of symbols and the desacralization of (certain) human flesh. For the Stars and Stripes and the mug shot of "Willie" Horton suggested powerful themes and related strategies in the 1988 election. Like my nightmare of "the culture, Stupid" as an actual road sign for the right, the flag-fetishism of '88 has also been literalized, as recent legislation proceeded to enact the already painfully literal statement made by George Bush's campaign appearance at an actual flag factory. Electoral imagery occupies a cultural space that at first glimpse seems quite distant from that of the academy, so in "Waving the Flag," I attempted to bridge this gap by connecting the censorship of free expression in the case of both the flag and the arts with the attack on "political correctness," particularly as manifested in university speech codes. The juxtaposition made it possible to argue that it was the real censors who were calling *us* censors.

But the culture war has so many fronts and so many battle-grounds within them—from library holdings to sex education classes to commercial television and film—and the manifestations of the flag wavers' zeal are often so grotesque that the university and the debates within and about it begin to seem, by comparison, like sheltered terrain. By concentrating on developments in or involving higher education, I may seem to be avoiding some of the sillier but also more effective aspects of the cultural campaign from the right. It seems to me, however, that, although the struggle for the university may be waged, in the first instance, on somewhat higher ground, the larger culture wars constitute their inevitable point of reference and their definitive context.

In March 1994, I spoke at an open hearing of my local public library board on the issue of retaining the book *Daddy's Roommate* in the children's section. (This slender volume, about a little boy whose divorced father is now part of a gay couple, has joined its more daring lesbian counterpart, *Heather Has Two Mommies*, in the canon of texts repeatedly targeted for censorship.) Identifying myself as a literature professor, I explained that I had nonetheless learned most of what I know about juvenile literature through the experience of raising my son. When Alex was three or four, I explained, we used to talk a lot about "dumb ideas"—shorthand for "dumb ideas about women and men," the attitudes that adult discourse calls sexism. "That sounds kind of dumb-ideasy," he'd say, sometimes adding, "That's a lie, isn't it?" He'd often come home from preschool with ideas whose dumbness he wanted to check on: women can't be doctors, only nurses; men don't cook dinner, and so on. And I always confirmed his sense that that was a lie, all right. Until one day he came to me indignant at the assertion that two men couldn't marry one another. "Well, no, that isn't a lie. But it *is* a dumb idea." Instead of stopping there, I went on to explain that they could love each other and live together, but they couldn't get married. And that it was called a gay relationship.

Why had I volunteered this additional information? And why was I now recounting the scene to an audience whose right wing used *its* children as props during their own frightened and frightening diatribes? It was because I knew my son was going to go on to grade school, middle school, high school, and hear more dumb ideas about homosexuality from his classmates, from all those boys whose first line of attack is "Faggot, faggot, faggot!" That's hate language, I told them, and before my kid was exposed to it, I wanted to be sure he had some love language in his head.

In a letter to the editor, I followed up this speech by addressing an argument to which the opponents of *Daddy's Roommate* gave great weight: since sodomy is illegal in that state, countenancing the book would be encouraging children to "pick and choose" among the laws to respect and those to ignore. Someday, I said, sodomy will no longer be illegal in Virginia, and when the law is changed it will be by people who *did* "pick and choose," people who were free to read—to read the Bible and *Daddy's Roommate*, King's "Letter from Birmingham Jail," Thoreau's "Civil Disobedience," and Baldwin's *Another Country*. (Always provide reading lists. You never know when someone is hearing about these books for the first time.)

The library board remained adamant in its support of the freedom to read and the right moved on to attack the composition of the board and the continued funding of the public libraries. This progression, with its increased abstraction from the (bland and unthreatening) content of *Daddy's Roommate* or the experience of reading it, taught me a great deal about the forms the culture war assumes in the world outside the academy. Meanwhile, inside the ivory tower, my department was in the final stages (or was it throes?) of its debate on the adoption of a new, "culture studies approach" to the first-year composition curriculum. The graduate students enrolled in my seminar on feminist critical theory were already teaching that curriculum to bemused and often hostile undergraduates. In papers for my graduate class, our theoretical readings, positing a feminism that connected gender to class and race, were the lens through which my students read their own attempts to be feminist teachers of writing, empowering undergraduates by helping them to analyze and critique complex texts about real-life social issues. They were very serious and very brave.

The night after my appearance at the library board, having spent part of my office hour composing the letter to the editor, I began my seminar by telling the students about the hearing. (It's a small town: a number of them had already heard reports.) Precisely because they were teaching a curriculum in rhetoric that confronted issues of racism and sexism, I thought it was important for them to know about the pressures against such a curriculum— or at least the spirit that informed it—within our own community, pressures that had contributed to the mentality of their undergraduate students. There were a few things I had learned about public speaking in such a context that I wanted to pass on—only in part because their rhetorical studies alerted them to the questions of "audience" and "reception" involved in my performance. Since we were studying theory, moreover, issues of value were central to our own work, and a book like *Daddy's Roommate*, which was a "text," but by no means a work of literature, helped to clarify them.

More typically, the aesthetics we discussed in the course would have us considering Maya Angelou versus Robert Frost as inaugural icons, considering on what grounds most of us would agree that Frost is the better writer and why I—and, I suspect, most of them—would maintain that Toni Morrison is better than either.

That rare confluence of the poet as speaking subject with political ritual also provided the occasion to ponder the way that Frost and Angelou were both eminently *safe* choices for their respective moments, and, from there, the question of what cultural "safety" in fact means. With John Kennedy's name firmly attached to Washington's major performing arts complex and with the Arts and Humanities Endowments associated with his administration's cultural patronage already under attack for venturing into territory decidedly less safe than Camelot, this was another place where literary theory might impinge on the real world.

In a sense, though, *Daddy's Roommate* and Angelou's inaugural performance were present in our classroom because I brought them there. And I did so, ironically, because the seminar was a safe place for me to connect my (far from epic) encounter with the Christian Coalition and its epigones to the themes of the course. Yet, a few weeks later, once it had been determined by departmental vote that, henceforth, the common first-year syllabus would address racial and gender differences as central categories for writing, once I was raising those same issues in a course on feminist critical theory, we at the university were opening ourselves to attack from the same forces that went after Daddy's poor queer roommate. Our undergraduate students, after all, were their children, too. From this perspective, the retreat to the classroom is at best a temporary withdrawal, fostering the illusion that it will always be up to me to select which elements of the real world I want to invite in.

I said that those graduate students were brave, meaning to honor their conviction that teaching undergraduates to write meant teaching them to write *something*—not, as Linda Brodkey puts it, to treat "writing as an intransitive verb"—and that the process entails confronting forces operating in the world outside the classroom.[1] In voluntarily effecting—what am I saying? in enthusiastically embracing—this confrontation, these graduate teaching assistants were exhibiting a kind of courage that was not demanded of me when I was in their place. By contrast, they were—or at least felt—called upon to display a level of prudence that was beyond my experience and, probably, my powers.

In the absence of the social movements that sustained me, my graduate students had no choice but to short-circuit what they read about race and gender back into the writing classroom. Not only was there no obvious movement on the national or international scene, no community organizing effort that would engage the energies aroused by literature and theory and cultural studies, but they found it difficult even to imagine such a development. (Significantly, only the foreign student in the class, who came from a repressive third world country, had encountered Marxist texts before and felt herself to be part of a social struggle whose primary venue was *not* the academy and its disciplines.)

An even more disturbing corollary is that these students, although radicalized by literature and theory and thus especially susceptible to the characteristic American tendency to translate politics into culture and thence, almost immediately, into personality, seemingly found it impossible to apply their politics to their own experience. No collective student voice was raised against the sexual harassment of women graduate students and young instructors or against an environment hostile to the hiring or retention of feminist faculty. The atmosphere in that department was very tense, leading students to assume that the slightest display of resistance would jeopardize their future. Their classmate who was returning to real and arbitrary tyranny in her own country had a more realistic sense of the possibilities as well as the dangers of collective action. And she was much bolder in imagining her own limits.

What I find especially sinister is, first of all, the American students' readiness to assume the worst about their situation and hence their acquiescence to authority *before* any pressure had been applied. And, beyond that, the fact that it was their very professionalism, which I now can't help seeing as premature rather than precocious, that made it impossible for them to take action on their own behalf or (say) mine. It is this professionalism that suggests the eventual success of a right-wing assault on the academy.

My fear is rooted in the way that the university has simultaneously been marginal and central to the culture wars in American society. A first inkling of this peculiar duality occurred just after the publication of E. D. Hirsch's *Cultural Literacy*, when, within a couple of months of each other, two different colleges invited me to debate Hirsch, then subsequently informed me that he had declined the invitation. Before I could begin secretly flexing my muscles before the mirror, exulting that Hirsch must be *afraid* to confront me (or, alternatively, before I could start resenting his summary dismissal of an antagonist too obscure to bother with), my hosts at the second institution told me Hirsch's office had explained that he no longer lectured on this topic at universities, but only in "the community." Since the thesis of *Cultural Literacy*—and, to an extent, the cult-lit industry the book spawned—had to do with the internal life of the community as a whole, I acknowledged the appropriateness of moving the debate to other sites. But it was impossible to ignore the fact that, in those other sites—libraries, public school systems, radio, TV, and magazine interviews—Hirsch's role was that of distinguished expert. He brought the prestige garnered by his academic writings and his chair at the University of Virginia, along with the éclat of best-sellerdom, into an arena where he faced no challengers with university credentials. No veteran of the campus debates was admitted there to point out the raw fact of dominance underlying the rhetoric of intra-cultural communication. Rather, the university was constructed as the source of Hirsch's authority but, also, at the same time, the source of our common cultural plight.

Similarly, in a number of more incendiary situations, the university is written out of the debate as being (always already) irremediably corrupted, as soon as academics bring into it the tradition of critical inquiry written into their job description. For instance, the National History Standards commissioned by Lynne Cheney and repudiated by her as soon as they were issued provided the by-now ex-Director of N.E.H. with the occasion to assault the Endowment with intent to kill. Cheney's own attitude and the media's representation of it both focused on the standards' "negativity," their "bashing" of America. In fact, it was the proposal's strengths that were targeted: its inclusion of social history and its emphasis on problematic moments in the national narrative, moments that could properly be subjected to historical debate. This approach to what young Americans should be taught about their country's past was rejected by Cheney and her media supporters in favor of what "everyone" already knows is most important about that history, even though the standards had been commissioned because "we" are insufficiently informed about our history. In a very real sense, the new standards were discredited in the public eye precisely because they had been drawn up by historians.

Similarly, the dispute over the Smithsonian's exhibit featuring the *Enola Gay* on the fiftieth anniversary of that plane's inaugurating the nuclear age over Hiroshima and Nagasaki, pitted fifty intervening years of debate about the decision to drop the bomb against the views of war veterans who believed that their own sacrifices and those of their dead comrades could be honored only by retroactive endorsement of war strategy, as well as war goals. The debate was often characterized as setting "history" against "memory," but what was actually being evoked in the arguments of official veterans' organizations was not their own counter-memory, but their personal investment in an uncritical narrative. Ultimately, the bowdlerized *Enola Gay* exhibit focused on the plane itself as a technological artifact while "historian" once again became an epithet synonymous with "detractor" and, of course, "elitist."

The accusation of elitism has the same resonance in the mouths of the powerful as censorship does in the rhetoric of the flag-idolaters. Expertise based on serious study is rejected precisely because it makes a claim to knowledge, but it is even more vulnerable if it acknowledges multiple sources of authority suggesting conflicting and debatable conclusions. In the case of the National History Standards, elitism apparently means attempting to expand the definition of history by including mass as well as elite experience. Recognizing the silenced voices of the oppressed—through newly uncovered written sources, material history, and oral interviews— is called elitist because it points to a less homogeneous and self-congratulatory national narrative. So doing people's history and asserting new knowledge on the basis of it is "elitist." Conversely, the belief that the veterans of a particular war are not the sole credible repository of knowledge about the conduct of that war—much less of the half-century's doomsday "peace" that has succeeded it— is equally elitist. Here, elitism means questioning the decisions of those in power.

The source of the historians' despised expertise is almost invariably the academy, which is the site of their training, the sponsor of much of their research, the home of some archival and documentary resources, and the locale where they or others of their ilk disseminate the information and methods that call received verities into question and thus redefine historical knowledge. In this understanding of the university's relation to historical scholarship, the institution is understood to be discredited from the outset, not only as the scene of all that teaching and research, but also as the *fons et origo* of multiculturalism, political correctness, feminism, deconstruction, postmodernism, and God only knows what other suspect fads.

Although the university is represented, in one sense, as being long-since lost to those demonic forces, it sometimes also appears as the virgin territory to be protected from invasion by them. When the curriculum becomes a public matter, as something still open to debate, the opinions of those previously assumed to hold a (wicked) hegemony are immediately marginalized. Astonishingly, the multiculturalists (politically correct, feminists, deconstructionists) are capable of already exercising virtually unlimited control while still seeking to take over. Witness the campaign orchestrated in 1990 by a small minority of the University of Texas English faculty that called for cancellation of a proposed new composition course, "Writing about Difference," which had been created and approved through established academic procedures, on the grounds that it was "really" an indoctrination in multicultural and feminist ideology. The underlying assumptions of the campaign, at least in its public dimension, were that multiculturalism and feminism were bad developments, reflections of the closing of the American mind, that they already ran rampant throughout the UT curriculum, especially in English, and through the faculty who implemented that curriculum, but that, at the same time, it was possible to "save" the curriculum from invasion through the exercise of (uninformed) political pressure.[2]

The immediate effect of the successful campaign against English 306 was to radicalize the graduate students who were involved in planning the course and hence in the struggle for its adoption. They started out believing in the efficacy and importance, for entering college students, of learning to identify and construct arguments about social difference. But I suspect that the empowerment they envisaged for their students was personal, based in social awareness, perhaps, but not oriented toward social action. I don't believe they or anyone else in the project expected undergraduates to be radicalized by the course—much less "brainwashed." For the graduate students themselves, however, observing the dissemination of a Big Lie about something that they knew firsthand, coming to recognize the forces deployed against this single course led to precisely the process of making connections that is at the root of a radical education. A number of them got involved in the power-structure research that exposed the University's other reactionary ties, particularly to a multinational corporation, Freeport McMoran, involved in questionable environmental and labor practices from Louisiana to Indonesia and currently threatening Austin's own cherished Barton Springs with development and pollution. Although it did not become uniform policy, the syllabus they helped design continued to function in their own classrooms, while their academic research and writing put together theory about social forces with readings of both canonical and newly legitimized literary texts. They became real pros.

So why do I worry about the present generation of graduate students and the direction in which *their* professionalism may take them, the curriculum, and the institution of higher education itself? The Texas case was exceptional, I think, in that graduate students' professionalism actually was enhanced by the central role they had assumed in the curriculum transformation project, and was supported by internal departmental procedures and majority faculty opinion. Although they were exposed to a media storm and consequent public outcry that far exceeded the expectations of even the most politically experienced faculty, not to mention the provocation offered by the revised composition syllabus, they were sheltered from its ugliest manifestations and possible consequences. They were not the ones who were personally vilified in newspapers statewide or the recipients of hate mail and harassing or threatening phone calls. Nor were their careers as doctoral candidates or future professors being put in jeopardy. They were thus in a position to cross over the threshold of the composition classroom and learn about the larger politics in which the university was invested, without the first "lesson's" consisting of discovering their own incalculable vulnerability. Intentionally or not, that cohort of Texas students received a crash course in educational politics without being forced to fill the role of crash course dummies.

More than five years later, the picture looks considerably grimmer. The media assault on (a still misinterpreted) "political correctness" has lost none of its energy or venom, and attacks on research, teaching loads, or employment of graduate assistants have been added to the mix, even when there has been little move toward curriculum transformation. A tenured faculty member spending only six hours a week in the classroom and devoting the rest of the work week to class preparation, student conferences, and research—in whatever proportions this division occurs and whatever the content of the research—is represented as being paid a full-time wage for part-time labor.

In this vein, an Associated Press series that ran in a number of Virginia newspapers in the fall of 1993 went so far as to ridicule particular faculty projects and dictate an alternative research agenda for the humanities. The principal thrust of these articles was that faculty at the lesser public institutions (everywhere but the University of Virginia at Charlottesville) ought to be teaching four to five courses a term, so the *ideal* research agenda was blank. Naming the topics, with their polysyllabic titles, on which faculty had worked instead of following that vacant agenda was inferentially equivalent to reducing them to absurdity. An English professor at Virginia Commonwealth University, for instance, had apparently wasted her time publishing a book on the representation of women in Trollope's parliamentary novels. This was understood to be an endeavor suitable only for the denizens of Laputa. (In fact, it seems to me that the series itself showed how useful it might be to trace back through the Victorians the ideological roots of the assumption that anything concerning women must be trivial.) The offense, in this case, was aggravated by the fact that no one in her department, that year, had published an article on methods of teaching grammar or Shakespeare! The only appropriate research, according to the AP, is about pedagogy and the journalists were sure they knew where said pedagogy should be directed—to a college English curriculum centered on grammar and Shakespeare.

Still, however influential the AP series may have been in preparing the ground for Virginia's slashing of its education budget, its rhetoric had only an indirect effect on educational policy. By contrast, as state legislatures and the trustees or regents of public universities begin to micro-manage labor, admissions, and curricular policy on campus, backed by newly organized reactionary alumni, pronouncements about "standards" and "the basics" are inevitably followed by efforts to restrict enrollment and roll the curriculum back into its traditional, pre-1970 boundaries. The English professor, whether as educator or specialist in literature, theory, or composition, has about as much credibility in this discourse as the historian does in the debate over the National History Standards or the *Enola Gay* exhibit. Our professionalism is irrelevant.

When I take umbrage at this irrelevance and yet express concern over the premature professionalism of today's graduate students, I am not contradicting *myself* so much as stumbling over two contradictory uses of the term. Insofar as the graduate students' experience as teachers of composition is informed by their commitment to teaching writing as a way of teaching critical thinking about central cultural themes, professionalism is synonymous with a desire to do good work in the world. The professionalism of mature academics (the kind I said was marginalized by university regents who wish to teach the canon and, within *it*, to rescue Jane Austen from feminist clutches) is based on that same desire, along with whatever the long years of marching through the institution have added. Were it not for my ongoing struggle with the secular fundamentalists on the question of making sacred texts out of canonical literature, I'd be tempted to call this "good" professionalism a sense of vocation.

More important than what we call it, however, is the fact that it is counterbalanced—if not, indeed, outweighed—by professionalism in the pejorative sense. I mean by this the deformations occurring in the present crop of graduate students in response to a grotesquely competitive labor market and the way that market is being exploited by those already established in the profession. The reduction of positions in the humanities, the creation of non–tenure track "visiting" assistant professorships to supplement the reliance on (also non-tenurable) full- and part-time lecturers, the repression of teaching-assistant unionization efforts, all contribute to a climate of insecurity in which the possibility of obtaining and holding on to the most mediocre of academic posts appears remote to a great many graduate students and recent Ph.Ds.[3] In this buyer's market, the requirements—always mechanically, quantitatively defined—are systematically raised at each level: M.A. students transferring to Ph.D.-granting institutions are expected to have delivered several conference papers to show their "professional" commitment and achievements, Ph.D candidates seeking an entry-level assistant professorship are expected to demonstrate scholarly promise by publishing at least a few articles, while candidates for tenure "need" at least one book and, very often, clearly defined publishing plans for a second one. As the ante goes up, nothing is said about the quality of the work being counted, much less about the writer's engagement and enthusiasm in its creation.

Inevitably, in these circumstances, those at the lower levels of the hierarchy come increasingly to understand "professionalization" as a function of production, without reference to content. Despite institutional rhetoric about interdisciplinarity and diversity, the job shortage also dictates specialization. At the entry level and in tenure decisions, the "field" tends to be defined in the least generous terms. Search committees use the dissertation topic as the sole guide to one's being "in" the (traditional) field for which they have advertised a "slot," while promotion committees discount publications in or even recommendations from fields outside that limited area.

The next step—opting for the "central" figures and traditional approaches to the "field"—has already begun. So that, even while feminist, multicultural, and queer studies are still part of the curriculum and still represent the cutting edge in scholarship, they are only sometimes defined as "fields" for recruitment in themselves, while still considered outside of the fields defined by period, nation, and genre. A reading of Victorian lesbian fiction would thus "belong" to feminist or gay studies, not to Victorian literature or the history of the novel—no matter how brilliantly it may challenge everything we thought we knew about either or both of these. Publishers may still prefer the ground-breaking study, but unemployment is hardly the most fertile ground for breaking ground, and the *threat* of unemployment, ironically enough, can be an even more potent silencer.

The graduate student who wants to be certified to take risks, both intellectual and political, in the classroom has to demonstrate that he or she is "safe" everywhere else, in matters of academic as well as of departmental discipline. In the '60s, quoting—in my case, unconsciously—C. Wright Mills, we used to say that tenure secured academic freedom for those who had sufficiently proved that they would not make use of it. It is getting to the point where that proof can be demanded earlier and oftener, which means that there are likely to be fewer young academics prepared to take those risks in the one site that they recognize as open to them. I certainly question the value of that classroom risk-taking in the absence not merely of the other kinds, but of a social movement to give meaning and direction to what happens in class. But the vision of a university without such critical classrooms is still more frightening.

March 3, 1996. I stopped at this point last night, planning to begin today's work by deciding whether the essay needed a further conclusion. This morning, I read the Sunday paper, the Raleigh, North Carolina, *News and Observer*, over breakfast. The stunningly mistitled "Insight" section reprints an article from *Congressional Quarterly* on the backlash against political correctness. After all this time, it appears that (unbeknownst to me) I and my kind do have hegemony after all. I delay my work brooding for an unconscionable time over each nutsy paragraph, until I realize that the article's saving grace is its self-contradictions. At one point, for instance, it describes the "problem" as a culture clash between increasingly conservative and career-minded undergraduates and the radicals from the '60s generation who have "assumed their places as tenured faculty." Yet a few inches down, the forces exerting pressure to "toe a leftist line" are enumerated: opinionated teachers, diversity-sensitive freshman orientations, and "militant groups of students [who] are said to create an atmosphere of intimidation that threatens even professors who fail to conform." (Must be those career-minded conservatives!) If this is their best rhetorical shot, maybe there's a chance that "It's the culture, Stupid," can still be a battle cry for both sides, not a death knell for critical intelligence.

NOTES

1. See "Not Just a Matter of Course: Lillian S. Robinson Talks with Linda Brodkey," *Women's Review of Books*, 9: 5 (February, 1992), 23.

2. In addition to my conversation with Brodkey, cited above, see Brodkey's longer account, "Making a Federal Case out of Difference: The Politics of Pedagogy, Publicity, and Postponement," in *Writing Theory and Critical Theory*, ed. John Clifford and John Schilb (New York: Modern Language Association, 1994), pp. 253–61; see also Brodkey's own book, *Writing Permitted in Designated Areas Only* (Minneapolis: University of Minnesota Press, 1996).

3. Unionization efforts among teaching assistants are heartening signs, even when, as in the case of the recent strike at Yale, the movement is defeated. In these times, I am also—albeit ironically—heartened by the way that, after the Yale strikers had been crushed, graduate students at other universities threatened to picket certain Yale faculty—the ones who had turned in their own TAs—when they came to their campuses for speaking engagements. Far from considering this militancy a manifestation of rampant know-nothingism, I believe it reflects a new generation's awareness that "progressive" research and writing is inadequate if unsupported by consistent action.

INDEX

LILLIAN S. ROBINSON, Professor of English at East Carolina University, has held teaching and research appointments at MIT, SUNY/Buffalo, the Sorbonne, Stanford, Wellesley, Tulsa, Albright, Scripps, San Diego State, Hawaii, Texas, and Virginia Tech. She is the author of *Sex, Class, and Culture* and *Monstrous Regiment*, a co-author of *Feminist Scholarship*, and editor of the four-volume *Modern Women Writers*.